EXPLORE
THE
TASTES
OF
MARYLAND

From the Mountains to the Sea

MARYLAND DIETETIC ASSOCIATION

Credits

Kari Beims, cover designer, is the founder of Dezining One, a visual communications design studio. Born and reared in Harford County, Maryland, she now lives in the Highlandtown neighborhood of Baltimore City. She received her B.A. in Art History and Studio Art from the University of Virginia, and a degree in Art Education from the University of North Carolina at Charlotte. In addition to being a graphic designer, Kari is also a painter, illustrator, sculptor, and a dedicated lover of fine cuisine— both cooking and eating.

EXPLORE THE TASTES OF MARYLAND
From the Mountains to the Sea

Designed, Edited, and Manufactured
By Favorite Recipes® Press
An imprint of

FRP™

P.O. Box 305142
Nashville, Tennessee 37230
1-800-358-0560

Art Director: Steve Newman
Cover Design: Kari Beims
Book Design: Dave Malone
Project Editor: Debbie Van Mol, R.D.

Manufactured in the United States of America
First Printing: 2002   6,000 copies

Contents

Preface

The Maryland Dietetic Association is delighted to present this collection of recipes for you. Our organization, which began as the Baltimore Dietetic Association in 1926 with only eleven members, today includes approximately 1,200 Registered Dietitians (RDs) and Registered Dietetic Technicians (DTRs). You will find us working throughout the state in various health, educational, and food service settings.

The development and publishing of this cookbook was undertaken to further our mission of "promoting optimal nutrition and well-being for all people." To do this we explored the varied cuisines of our state and gathered the favorite recipes of our members. We quickly saw that the recipes collected were as varied as the Maryland landscape. The resultant collection reflects the history, geography, and ethnicity of our members as well as the world in which we live today.

To publish a cookbook without consideration of this information would truly be remiss; so we have added sidebars including facts about our state, its history, and its people as well as quick nutrition facts and helpful cooking hints. Please note that we did not intend the cookbook to favor any one particular dietary focus. Rather, we believe in the philosophy that "all foods can fit." So you will notice that, while we have included some "lite fare" recipes, some others may have considerable amounts of fat, sugar, sodium, etc. When selecting such recipes, please consider how that particular dish fits into your daily diet so that you can maintain a healthy balance. A nutritional profile is included at the end of each recipe to help guide your choices. Sometimes the sidebar information will also suggest suitable ingredient substitutes.

And sometimes it's the creativity of the cook, not terrific culinary skills, which brings pleasure and satisfaction to the eater. Our section of children's recipes capitalizes on that creativity to make meals and snacks especially enjoyable for younger eaters. We hope you find our book adds to your culinary delight and is pleasurable to read!

Maryland Dietetic Association

Acknowledgments

COOKBOOK STEERING COMMITTEE

Co-chairs:
        Judith Dzimiera, MEd., RD, LD
        Marie DeMarco, MS, RD, LD

Marketing:
        Robin Thomas, MS, RD, LN

Recipe Selection:
        Carol Miller, MEd., RD, LD, Coordinator
        Kelly Harvey, MS, RD, LD, CDE, Southern Maryland
            Representative
        Nina Parks Hoy, MS, RD, LD, Eastern Shore Representative
        Jennifer Wilson, MEd., RD, LD, Western Area Representative

Non-recipe text: Marie DeMarco, MS, RD, LD
        Judith Dzimiera, MEd., RD, LD
        Roxanne Moore, MS, RD, LD
        Robin Thomas, MS, RD, LN
        Joanne Zacharias, MS, RD, LD

At-large:
        Lesa Amy, MS, RD
        Concepcion Placiente, MS, RD, LD
        Joanne Zacharias, MS, RD, LD

Cooking & Maryland—A Brief History

Maryland has often been called "America in Miniature," and a quick look at its geography will explain why. Our state spans 125 miles from north to south and 240 miles from east to west with the Chesapeake Bay in between. Its total area is about 12,300 square miles. On either side of the bay we have low-lying, flat coastal plain areas with light, sandy soils, and tide-covered marshes. In the colonial period, the coastal plain areas of both the Eastern and Western Shores were good for the growing of tobacco. Today, crops such as corn, soybeans, tomatoes, cucumbers, melons, and strawberries are produced. The coastal plain also provides homes for many deer, small animals, and a variety of waterfowl.

On our Eastern Shore there are many poultry farms. The watermen of the Bay harvest crabs, oysters, clams, and fish. West of the Bay and its coastal plain areas lie the low, rolling hills of the Piedmont Plateau. This area contains very fertile soil especially good for the growing of wheat and corn. Many commercial and residential farms are found in this area. Milk cows and thoroughbred horses are raised here too. Still farther west are the Appalachian Mountains with beautiful forests and valleys. There are many orchards in the western part of Maryland; livestock and dairy farms produce meat, milk, eggs, and butter.

And so, the geography of our state, moving from the coastal plain to the Piedmont Plateau to the mountains of the west, mimics the geography of the country, moving from the low, coastal cities of the Atlantic states, through the Mid-west to the Rockies and Sierra Nevada mountains. The geography of Maryland with its shores, plains, mountains, and our temperate climate provides us with the foodstuffs of healthy eating and truly makes it the "land of pleasant living."

If the heart of Maryland cooking lies in the varied geography of the land, then the soul of Maryland cooking lies in the history of its people. Maryland's first cooks were really the American Indians. Those first inhabitants of our land migrated from Asia across the Bering Strait to Alaska, then gradually made their way across North America, reaching the mid-Atlantic area about 10,000 years ago. In that time period, glaciers covered much of the states north of us, even reaching down to parts of western Maryland. And the Chesapeake Bay hadn't even been formed! In those days, the Indians of North America were hunters of fish and game animals and gatherers of nuts, seeds, and berries. These early American Indians were nomadic—living off the land—and moving from season to season in order to survive.

Eventually the climate warmed and the glaciers retreated northward. The melting of these glaciers raised sea level and created the Chesapeake Bay. Gradually forests replaced grasslands, and the American Indians adapted. Stone and oyster shells were used to make tools and bowls.

Food was cooked. Animal skins and bark from trees were used for shelters. By the 1600s, the American Indians continued to hunt and gather, but they had also learned to trap fish and shellfish and to grow their own food. They settled into small villages. It was the Algonquin Indians of this time who met the first settlers from England when the *Arc* and the *Dove* arrived in southern Maryland (St. Mary's City) in March 1634. Those American Indians taught the settlers how to farm the land by growing maize, beans, and squash. Amazingly, their influence can still be seen in Maryland cuisine today in dishes such as succotash, baked beans, and roasted corn.

The spirit of Maryland cooking lies in the ethnic diversity of its people. The 1600s saw English colonists arrive seeking religious freedom. In the early 1700s, Germans moved from York, Pennsylvania, seeking fertile farmland in Frederick. They tended livestock and planted apple, pear, and peach orchards. Among them were tanners, millers, and carpenters. They made and traded many goods formerly imported from Europe.

This increase in commerce forced the need for roads and helped to establish port cities such as Baltimore. Over the next hundred years, Maryland became a major center of commerce. Our port cities facilitated the exchange of people and commodities between North America and other parts of the world. The National Road, completed in 1818, connected Cumberland in Western Maryland with farmers of the Ohio Valley, making our state a gateway to the west. Stagecoaches, mail carriers, and large wagons carried wheat, cheeses, manufactured goods, and news to and from the frontier. Innkeepers of Western Maryland provided hearty meals and hospitality for travelers. The Chesapeake and Ohio Canal, completed in 1850, followed the Potomac River for over 180 miles through the Allegheny Mountains of Western Maryland connecting Georgetown to Cumberland. And the Baltimore & Ohio Railroad, completed by 1853, allowed passengers and goods from all over the country to reach Maryland's port cities.

Maryland's population grew rapidly in the 1800s. In fact, Locust Point in Baltimore was second only to Ellis Island in New York in the number of immigrants using it as a point of entry to the United States. Today, Maryland's population exceeds five million residents, and our state continues to be a major force in industry, commerce, agriculture, and tourism welcoming people with diverse ethnic backgrounds and their rich variety of food traditions.

The heart, soul, and spirit of Maryland cooking, our collection reflects the history, geography, and ethnicity of our fair state, its people, and the times in which we live.

Bon appétit!

Nutritional Guidelines

The editors have attempted to present these family recipes in a format that allows approximate nutritional values to be computed. Persons with dietary or health problems or whose diets require close monitoring should not rely solely on the nutritional information provided. They should consult their physician or a registered dietitian for specific information.

Nutritional information for these recipes is computed from information derived from many sources, including materials supplied by the United States Department of Agriculture, computer databanks, and journals in which the information is assumed to be in the public domain. However, many specialty items, new products, and processed foods may not be available from these sources or may vary from the average values used in these profiles. More information on new and/or specific products may be obtained by reading the nutrient labels. Unless otherwise specified, the nutritional profile of these recipes is based on all measurements being level.

- Artificial sweeteners vary in use and strength and should be used to taste, using the recipe ingredients as a guideline. Sweeteners using aspartame (NutraSweet® and Equal®) should not be used as a sweetener in recipes involving prolonged heating, which reduces the sweet taste. For further information on the use of these sweeteners, refer to the package.
- Alcoholic ingredients have been analyzed for the basic information. Cooking causes the evaporation of alcohol, which decreases alcoholic and caloric content.
- Buttermilk, sour cream, and yogurt are the types available commercially.
- Canned beans and vegetables have been analyzed with the canning liquid. Rinsing and draining canned products will lower the sodium content.
- Chicken, cooked for boning and chopping, has been roasted; this method yields the lowest caloric values.
- Cottage cheese is cream-style with 4.2% creaming mixture. Dry curd cottage cheese has no creaming mixture.
- Eggs are all large. To avoid raw eggs that may carry salmonella, as in eggnog or 6-week muffin batter, use an equivalent amount of pasteurized egg substitute.
- Fat content of ground beef is 16%; 10% for extra-lean ground beef.
- Flour is unsifted all-purpose flour.
- Garnishes, serving suggestions, and other optional information are not included in the profile.
- Margarine and butter are regular, not whipped or presoftened.
- Milk is whole milk, 3.5% butterfat. Low-fat milk is 1% butterfat. Evaporated milk is whole milk with 60% of the water removed.
- Oil is any type of vegetable cooking oil. Shortening is hydrogenated vegetable shortening.
- Ingredients to taste have not been included in the nutritional profile.
- If a choice of ingredients has been given, the profile reflects the first option. If a choice of amounts has been given, the profile reflects the greater amount.

Appetizers & Beverages

Appetizers & Beverages

Hot Broccoli Dip

1 (10-ounce) package frozen chopped broccoli, thawed
1/2 cup low-fat mayonnaise
1/2 cup fat-free sour cream
1/4 cup grated Parmesan cheese
2 tablespoons drained chopped roasted red peppers
1/8 teaspoon thyme
Garlic powder to taste
Hot sauce to taste

Drain the broccoli on a paper towel. Combine the broccoli, mayonnaise, sour cream, cheese, red peppers, thyme, garlic powder and hot sauce in a bowl and mix well. Spoon the broccoli mixture into a microwave-safe dish. Microwave on High for 6 minutes. Serve with thinly sliced toasted French bread and/or melba toast.

You may spoon the broccoli mixture into a baking dish and bake at 350 degrees for 30 minutes or until bubbly.

Makes 16 (2-tablespoon) servings

Nutrients Per Serving: Cal 37; Prot 2 g; Carbo 4 g; T Fat 2 g; (Saturated Fat 1 g); 45% Cal from Fat; Chol 3 mg; Fiber 1 g; Sod 84 mg; Calcium 36 mg

Broccoli is not only a member of the cabbage family, but is also considered a cruciferous vegetable. These cabbage family vegetables get their name from their four-petaled flowers, which look like a crucifix, or cross. Studies suggest that cabbage family vegetables may help protect against colon and rectal cancer. Experts believe that they contain nutrients and phytochemicals that have a cancer-fighting component known as beta carotene. Broccoli is also a good source of vitamin C and fiber.

Veggie Dip

1¹/₂ cups low-fat yogurt
¹/₂ cup lite mayonnaise
1 tablespoon drained capers
1 tablespoon minced fresh parsley (optional)
1 tablespoon grated onion
1 teaspoon Worcestershire sauce
¹/₂ teaspoon each basil, oregano and thyme
¹/₂ teaspoon salt
¹/₄ teaspoon curry powder

Combine the yogurt and mayonnaise in a bowl and mix well. Stir in the capers, parsley, onion, Worcestershire sauce, basil, oregano, thyme, salt and curry powder. Chill, covered, for 1 hour or longer.

Serve with carrot sticks, celery sticks, bell pepper chunks, jicama, snow peas, cherry tomatoes and/or any fresh vegetable of choice.

Makes 16 (2-tablespoon) servings

Nutrients Per Serving: Cal 40; Prot 1 g; Carbo 2 g; T Fat 3 g; (Saturated Fat 1 g); 63% Cal from Fat; Chol 4 mg; Fiber <1 g; Sod 168 mg; Calcium 43 mg

Vidalia Onion Dip

2 cups (8 ounces) shredded sharp Cheddar cheese
1 medium Vidalia onion, chopped
³/₄ cup mayonnaise

Combine the cheese, onion and mayonnaise in a food processor. Pulse just until blended; do not overprocess. Spoon the onion mixture into an 8x8-inch baking dish. Bake at 350 degrees for 25 minutes or until the edges are brown. Serve hot with chips and/or assorted party crackers.

Substitute Swiss cheese or hot Pepper Jack cheese for the Cheddar cheese for variety.

Serves 8

Nutrients Per Serving: Cal 269; Prot 7 g; Carbo 2 g; T Fat 26 g; (Saturated Fat 9 g); 87% Cal from Fat; Chol 45 mg; Fiber <1 g; Sod 288 mg; Calcium 206 mg

Dress up your dips with more than chips. Add some nutritious crunch with colorful carrots, celery, bell peppers, jicama, snow peas, or cherry tomatoes. This is a simple and easy way to add vitamin A and vitamin C to your diet.

Taco Dip

1 (16-ounce) can refried beans
8 to 16 ounces prepared
    guacamole
1 (4-ounce) can chopped black
    olives, drained
1/2 cup chopped fresh tomato

1/2 cup (2 ounces) shredded
    Cheddar cheese
1/2 cup (2 ounces) shredded
    Monterey Jack cheese
1/3 to 1/2 cup sour cream
1/2 cup chopped fresh tomato

Layer the beans, guacamole, olives, 1/2 cup chopped tomato, Cheddar cheese, Monterey Jack cheese and sour cream in the order listed on a decorative platter or in a shallow dish.

Sprinkle with 1/2 cup chopped tomato. Chill, covered, until serving time. Serve with tortilla chips.

Serves 8

Nutrients Per Serving: Cal 226; Prot 8 g; Carbo 15 g; T Fat 16 g; (Saturated Fat 6 g); 60% Cal from Fat; Chol 25 mg; Fiber 6 g; Sod 390 mg; Calcium 160 mg

Taco Salad Dip

2 cups nonfat plain yogurt
8 ounces nonfat cream cheese,
    softened
1 envelope taco seasoning mix
1 cup salsa
1/2 head iceberg lettuce,
    shredded

2 tomatoes, chopped
1/2 cup chopped scallions
1 cup (4 ounces) shredded
    Cheddar cheese
1 (4-ounce) can sliced black
    olives, drained

Beat the yogurt and cream cheese in a mixing bowl until smooth. Add the taco seasoning mix and mix well. Chill, covered, for 1 hour or longer. Spread the yogurt mixture over the bottom of a shallow round dish. Spread with the salsa. Top with the lettuce, tomatoes and scallions. Sprinkle with the Cheddar cheese and olives. Serve with baked tortilla chips, pita bread quarters or flour tortillas cut into eighths.

Serves 12

Nutrients Per Serving: Cal 106; Prot 8 g; Carbo 10 g; T Fat 4 g; (Saturated Fat 2 g); 36% Cal from Fat; Chol 12 mg; Fiber 1 g; Sod 482 mg; Calcium 198 mg

The avocado is a fruit with a rich, silken, buttery texture and a high fat content. However, the majority of the calories are heart-smart mono-unsaturated fats. Even though these fats are the better type, be sure to control your portion sizes so that the total amount of fat consumed is in check.

Jezebel Sauce

1 (18-ounce) jar apricot preserves
1 (18-ounce) jar apple jelly
3 tablespoons dry mustard
1/2 cup plus 2 tablespoons prepared horseradish
1 tablespoon pepper

Combine the preserves, jelly, dry mustard, prepared horseradish and pepper in a bowl and mix well. Store the sauce in an airtight container in the refrigerator until serving time.

To serve, spoon the sauce over softened cream cheese. Serve with assorted party crackers. You may freeze the sauce for future use if desired.

Makes 40 (2-tablespoon) servings

Nutrients Per Serving: Cal 75; Prot <1 g; Carbo 18 g; T Fat <1 g; (Saturated Fat 0 g); 4% Cal from Fat; Chol 0 mg; Fiber <1 g; Sod 23 mg; Calcium 7 mg

Many local churches have fund-raisers that sell foods prepared by Marylanders. Jezebel Sauce has been a hit at the Fallston Presbyterian Church Christmas Bazaar for the past ten years.

Curry Chive Mayonnaise

1/2 cup low-fat mayonnaise
1 tablespoon chives
1 teaspoon curry powder
1 teaspoon sherry vinegar
1/4 teaspoon salt
1/4 teaspoon pepper

Mix the mayonnaise, chives, curry powder, vinegar, salt and pepper in a bowl. Chill, covered, in the refrigerator until serving time. Serve with steamed shrimp or use as a spread on turkey sandwiches.

Makes 6 (1-tablespoon) servings

Nutrients Per Serving: Cal 68; Prot <1 g; Carbo 2 g; T Fat 7 g; (Saturated Fat 1 g); 87% Cal from Fat; Chol 7 mg; Fiber <1 g; Sod 256 mg; Calcium 3 mg

Spinach and Artichoke Spread

1 (10-ounce) package frozen chopped spinach, thawed
1 (14-ounce) can artichoke hearts, drained, chopped
3/4 cup (3 ounces) freshly grated Parmesan cheese
1/2 cup mayonnaise
1/2 cup sour cream
Pepper to taste

Press the excess moisture from the spinach. Combine the spinach, artichokes, cheese, mayonnaise and sour cream in a bowl and mix gently. Season with pepper.

Spoon the spinach mixture into an 8-inch baking dish. Bake at 350 degrees for 15 to 20 minutes or until heated through. Serve hot with assorted party crackers, party bread and/or fresh vegetables.

Serve as an appetizer or as an accompaniment to soups and salads. Use lite or fat-free mayonnaise and sour cream to reduce the fat grams.

Serves 10

Nutrients Per Serving: Cal 160; Prot 5 g; Carbo 6 g; T Fat 13 g; (Saturated Fat 4 g); 72% Cal from Fat; Chol 18 mg; Fiber 2 g; Sod 440 mg; Calcium 127 mg

Spinach and Artichoke Spread was a definite favorite among our taste testers! Try this at your next party. Serve with assorted party crackers or toasted pita bread wedges.

Crab Meat Spread

1 pound backfin crab meat, shells removed and flaked
2 cups mayonnaise
1/2 (3-ounce) bottle capers, rinsed, drained
3/4 cup shredded Swiss, mozzarella or Cheddar cheese

Combine the crab meat, mayonnaise and capers in a bowl and mix well. Spoon the crab meat mixture into a round baking dish. Sprinkle with the cheese. Bake at 350 degrees until light brown and bubbly. Serve hot with assorted party crackers, chips, corn chips and/or bread cubes. Add chopped onion and/or Old Bay seasoning for variety.

Serves 16

Nutrients Per Serving: Cal 220; Prot 2 g; Carbo <1 g; T Fat 23 g; (Saturated Fat 5 g); 96% Cal from Fat; Chol 25 mg; Fiber 0 g; Sod 221 mg; Calcium 50 mg

Patuxent Marinated Crab Meat

*The Patuxent River is
the longest river that is
entirely contained
within the state of
Maryland. Patuxent
River State Park,
located along the
upper twelve miles of
the river in Howard
and Montgomery
counties, offers
hunting, fishing, hiking,
and horseback riding.*

1 pound fresh or pasteurized Maryland crab meat
1/3 cup finely chopped onion
1/2 cup cider vinegar
1/4 cup vegetable oil
1/4 cup water
1 tablespoon Old Bay seasoning
1 tablespoon chopped fresh parsley

Remove any shell and cartilage from the crab meat. Combine the crab meat and onion in a glass or plastic bowl and mix gently.

Whisk the vinegar, oil, water, Old Bay seasoning and parsley in a bowl until mixed. Add the vinaigrette to the crab meat mixture and mix gently. Marinate, covered with plastic wrap, in the refrigerator for 2 hours or longer. Serve with assorted party crackers.

Serves 4

Nutrients Per Serving: Cal 287; Prot 22 g; Carbo 3 g; T Fat 21 g; (Saturated Fat 3 g); 65% Cal from Fat; Chol 107 mg; Fiber <1 g; Sod 857 mg; Calcium 119 mg

Hot and Cheesy Crab Dip

3/4 cup mayonnaise
3/4 cup (3 ounces) shredded Cheddar cheese
1 1/2 teaspoons Old Bay seasoning
1 teaspoon Worcestershire sauce
1/4 teaspoon dry mustard
1 pound fresh lump crab meat, shells and cartilage removed
3/4 cup (3 ounces) shredded Cheddar cheese
1/8 teaspoon Old Bay seasoning

Combine the mayonnaise, 3/4 cup cheese, 1 1/2 teaspoons Old Bay seasoning, Worcestershire sauce and dry mustard in a bowl and mix well. Fold in the crab meat.

Spoon the crab meat mixture into a 1-quart baking dish. Sprinkle with 3/4 cup cheese and 1/8 teaspoon Old Bay seasoning. Bake at 350 degrees for 12 to 15 minutes or until brown around the edges. Serve hot with pita chips and/or assorted party crackers.

Makes 24 (2-tablespoon) servings

Nutrients Per Serving: Cal 79; Prot 2 g; Carbo <1 g; T Fat 8 g; (Saturated Fat 2 g); 90% Cal from Fat; Chol 13 mg; Fiber 0 g; Sod 130 mg; Calcium 52 mg

Even newcomers to Baltimore quickly learn that both crab meat and Old Bay seasoning are essential to Maryland cuisine!

Maryland Crab Dip

16 ounces lite cream cheese, softened
2 tablespoons Old Bay seasoning
2 tablespoons prepared horseradish
2 tablespoons Worcestershire sauce
1 garlic clove, minced
1 (12-ounce) can evaporated skim milk
2 tablespoons lemon juice
1 pound fresh crab meat, shells and cartilage removed
1/4 cup grated fat-free Parmesan cheese
1/4 cup shredded low-fat Cheddar cheese

Combine the cream cheese, Old Bay seasoning, prepared horseradish, Worcestershire sauce and garlic in a mixing bowl. Beat until creamy, scraping the bowl occasionally. Add the evaporated skim milk and lemon juice and beat until blended. Fold in the crab meat.

Spoon the crab meat mixture into an 8x8-inch baking dish. Sprinkle the Parmesan cheese and Cheddar cheese over the top. Bake at 350 degrees for 12 minutes. Serve hot with crusty French bread.

Serves 12

Nutrients Per Serving: Cal 95; Prot 8 g; Carbo 7 g; T Fat 4 g; (Saturated Fat 2 g); 35% Cal from Fat; Chol 16 mg; Fiber <1 g; Sod 591 mg; Calcium 145 mg

Many recipes special to our region, including this appetizer, use Maryland in the title. One of the thirteen original colonies, our state was named for Queen Henrietta Maria, the wife of Charles I of England. As translated "Terra Mariae" means Mary's Land, or Maryland.

Maryland Clams Casino

12 fresh cherrystone clams in shells
1 to 2 drops of Worcestershire sauce
1 to 2 drops of hot sauce
3 slices partially cooked bacon, drained, cut into fourths
Seasoned bread crumbs to taste

Open the clam shells, allowing the clam to remain on one half and discarding the remaining half. Arrange the shells clam side up in a shallow baking pan. Top each clam with Worcestershire sauce and hot sauce. Sprinkle with the bacon and bread crumbs.

Broil the clams 4 inches from the heat source for 2 to 3 minutes or until the edges of the clams curl and the bacon is cooked through.

Makes 12 appetizers

Nutrients Per Serving: Cal 41; Prot 4 g; Carbo 1 g; T Fat 2 g; (Saturated Fat 1 g); 54% Cal from Fat; Chol 10 mg; Fiber 0 g; Sod 56 mg; Calcium 13 mg

Clams are available year-round. Purchase them live in the shell, fresh shucked, frozen, canned, or breaded. When buying clams in the shell, as for this recipe, be sure they are alive and fresh. Touch the siphon; it should retract. Then place the clams in a container of fresh water and add a small amount of cornmeal. Let stand for a few hours. This process gives the clams a chance to expel any sand they may have ingested before harvest.

Crab Melt-Aways

1 (7-ounce) can crab meat, drained
8 ounces Cheddar cheese, shredded
1/4 cup (1/2 stick) margarine, softened
2 tablespoons mayonnaise
1 teaspoon prepared mustard (optional)
1/2 teaspoon seasoned salt (optional)
1/2 teaspoon garlic powder
6 English muffins, split
1 cucumber, thinly sliced

Rinse the crab meat gently and drain on a paper towel. Combine the crab meat, cheese, margarine, mayonnaise, prepared mustard, seasoned salt and garlic powder in a bowl and mix well. Spread the crab meat mixture on the cut sides of the muffins.

Arrange the muffin halves cut side up on a baking sheet. Broil until bubbly and brown. Serve immediately with cucumber slices. May be prepared in advance, covered with plastic wrap and frozen unbaked for future use.

Makes 1 dozen melt-aways

Nutrients Per Serving: Cal 214; Prot 11 g; Carbo 14 g; T Fat 13 g; (Saturated Fat 5 g); 53% Cal from Fat; Chol 36 mg; Fiber 1 g; Sod 362 mg; Calcium 209 mg

Crab meat is available in the following forms: Lump is the most expensive and consists of the largest pieces from the body adjacent to the backfin; use it where appearance is important, such as in a crab salad or Crab Imperial (page 109). Backfin consists of lump and some flakes; use it for crab cakes and Crab Imperial. Special consists of flakes of white body meat without the lump; use for soups, casseroles, or dips. Claw is brownish meat from the claws; use for soups, crab balls, or dips.

Rosemary-Skewered Shrimp

3 pounds large shrimp, peeled, deveined
1 cup olive oil
8 garlic cloves, crushed
16 long rosemary branches
Salt and pepper to taste

Arrange the shrimp in a single layer in a shallow glass or plastic dish. Combine the olive oil and garlic in a bowl and mix well. Pour the olive oil mixture over the shrimp, turning to coat. Marinate, covered with plastic wrap, in the refrigerator for 2 hours, turning occasionally; drain.

Soak the rosemary branches in water in a shallow dish for 1 hour; drain. Remove the leaves from the ends of the rosemary branches and shape the ends of each branch with a sharp knife into a point to form a skewer.

Thread 3 or 4 shrimp on each rosemary skewer. Sprinkle the shrimp with salt and pepper. Grill over medium-high heat for 3 to 5 minutes per side or until the shrimp turn pink.

Makes 8 (2-skewer) servings

Nutrients Per Serving: Cal 346; Prot 22 g; Carbo 1 g; T Fat 28 g; (Saturated Fat 4 g); 73% Cal from Fat; Chol 202 mg; Fiber <1 g; Sod 232 mg; Calcium 46 mg
Nutritional profile includes all of the ingredients.

Rosemary is in the mint family of herbs. Its name comes from the Latin for "sea dew," and refers to the fact that it is often found growing along the seacoast. Use herbs and spices to season and enhance the flavor of your foods without the addition of salt.

Maryland Terrapin

1 tablespoon brown flour
1 cup (2 sticks) butter, cut into chunks
1 tablespoon sugar
1 teaspoon nutmeg
1/8 teaspoon ground cloves
Salt and pepper to taste
Juice of 1 large lemon
1 quart chopped terrapin meat
Sherry to taste

Place the brown flour in a cast-iron skillet. Stir in the butter, sugar, nutmeg, cloves, salt, pepper and lemon juice in the order listed. Add the terrapin and mix well. Cook until heated through, stirring frequently. Drizzle with sherry just before serving.

To prepare the terrapin, place the terrapin in a large container of water for 8 to 10 hours to cleanse; drain. Place the terrapin in a large stockpot. Add enough boiling water to cover. Cook for 1 1/2 hours or until the nails are easily removed. Pick the meat from the bones, being careful not to puncture the gall. Reserve all the eggs.

Serves 9

Nutrients Per Serving: Cal 290; Prot 15 g; Carbo 3 g; T Fat 25 g; (Saturated Fat 14 g); 76% Cal from Fat; Chol 92 mg; Fiber <1 g; Sod 301 mg; Calcium 94 mg

The diamond-back terrapin was once so plentiful in the Chesapeake Bay, Turtle Soup was the common food for the poor and slaves. Today, because of its relative scarcity, it is considered a luxury and is served in appetizer portions. Note the historical nature of this recipe—included here for the adventurous cook!

Miniature Egg Rolls

1 pound ground pork
4 ounces chopped peeled shrimp
1/4 cup finely chopped onion
1/4 cup finely chopped celery
2 tablespoons cornstarch
1 egg, beaten
2 teaspoons finely crushed garlic
Salt and pepper to taste
35 spring roll wrappers
1 egg, beaten
Vegetable oil for deep-frying

Combine the ground pork, shrimp, onion, celery, cornstarch, 1 egg, garlic, salt and pepper in a bowl and mix well. Place 1 tablespoon of the pork filling 1 inch from the edge of each spring roll wrapper and spread the filling lengthwise. Roll to enclose the filling.

Brush the edges with 1 beaten egg to seal. Deep-fry the egg rolls in 375-degree oil until brown on all sides; drain. Serve with sweet-and-sour sauce.

Makes 35 egg rolls

Nutrients Per Serving: Cal 131; Prot 7 g; Carbo 19 g; T Fat 3 g; (Saturated Fat 1 g);
19% Cal from Fat; Chol 30 mg; Fiber 1 g; Sod 201 mg; Calcium 20 mg
Nutritional profile reflects the substitution of egg roll wrappers for spring roll wrappers.
Nutritional profile does not include vegetable oil for deep-frying.

Many people avoid Oriental foods because of the sodium content. This recipe is low in sodium because of the use of fresh vegetables and pepper instead of soy sauce and salt.

Sugar and Spice Nuts

1 tablespoon margarine, melted
1 egg white, lightly beaten
2 cups unroasted almonds, English walnuts or pecans
1 cup sugar
1 1/2 teaspoons cinnamon
3/4 teaspoon each nutmeg and allspice
1/2 teaspoon salt

Add the margarine to the egg white gradually, stirring constantly. Fold in the almonds. Mix the remaining ingredients in a bowl. Spread about 1/4 of the sugar mixture in a 10x15-inch baking pan. Coat the almonds in batches in the remaining sugar mixture and arrange in a single layer in the prepared pan. Sprinkle with the sugar mixture. Bake at 300 degrees for 15 minutes or until the almonds are light brown. Remove from oven and stir gently. Let stand until cool. Store the almonds in a container with a tight-fitting lid.

Makes 16 (1/4-cup) servings

Nutrients Per Serving: Cal 158; Prot 4 g; Carbo 16 g; T Fat 10 g; (Saturated Fat 1 g); 52% Cal from Fat; Chol 0 mg; Fiber 2 g; Sod 85 mg; Calcium 45 mg

Hot-or-Cold Tomato Beef Beverage

1 (46-ounce) can vegetable juice cocktail
1 (10-ounce) can beef consommé
1/3 cup orange juice
1 teaspoon Worcestershire sauce
1/2 teaspoon onion salt
1/4 teaspoon black pepper, or 1/3 teaspoon white pepper

Combine all the ingredients in a large container and mix well. Let stand at room temperature for 1 hour or longer to allow the flavors to marry.

To serve cold, pour over ice in glasses. Garnish with sprigs of fresh parsley or celery leaves. To serve hot, heat for 20 minutes in a saucepan. Ladle into mugs. Garnish with lemon slices.

Makes 10 (6-ounce) servings

Nutrients Per Serving: Cal 36; Prot 2 g; Carbo 7 g; T Fat <1 g; (Saturated Fat <1 g); 3% Cal from Fat; Chol 0 mg; Fiber 1 g; Sod 603 mg; Calcium 18 mg

Hot-or-Cold Tomato Beef Beverage is great as a refreshing drink in the summer and warm and cozy as an appetizer beverage when the weather is chilly!

Vitamin C Breeze

1 3/4 cups chopped cantaloupe, chilled
1 cup chopped kiwifruit, chilled
1 cup orange sherbet

Combine the cantaloupe, kiwifruit and sherbet in a food processor. Process until smooth. Pour into glasses.

Makes 2 (1 1/4-cup) servings

Nutrients Per Serving: Cal 204; Prot 3 g; Carbo 47 g; T Fat 2 g; (Saturated Fat 1 g); 9% Cal from Fat; Chol 4 mg; Fiber 4 g; Sod 51 mg; Calcium 78 mg

Bourbon Slushies

10 cups water
5 tea bags
2 cups sugar
1 1/2 cups bourbon
1 (12-ounce) can frozen orange juice concentrate
1 (6-ounce) can frozen lemonade concentrate

Bring the water to a boil in a nonreactive pan. Remove from heat. Add the tea bags. Steep for 3 to 4 minutes. Discard the tea bags. Stir in the sugar. Add the bourbon, orange juice concentrate and lemonade concentrate and mix well.

Let stand until cool. Pour the bourbon mixture into a freezer container. Freeze for 8 to 10 hours or until beginning to get firm; stir. Spoon into glasses.

Serves 18

Nutrients Per Serving: Cal 177; Prot <1 g; Carbo 34 g; T Fat <1 g; (Saturated Fat <1 g); 0% Cal from Fat; Chol 0 mg; Fiber <1 g; Sod 5 mg; Calcium 7 mg

Vitamin C Breeze features kiwifruit, which is the berry of a woody vine native to China. Even though it has a "homely" appearance because of its hairy, dull brown covering, the kiwifruit contains seventy-four milligrams of vitamin C.

Classic Black-Eyed Susan

1 ounce (2 tablespoons) rum
1 ounce (2 tablespoons) vodka
3/4 ounce (1¹/2 tablespoons) Cointreau
1 lime wedge
¹/4 cup orange juice
¹/4 cup pineapple juice

Mix the rum, vodka and liqueur in a shaker. Squeeze the juice from the lime wedge into the rum mixture. Add the orange juice and pineapple juice and shake to mix. Pour over crushed ice in a glass.

Serves 1

Nutrients Per Serving: Cal 220; Prot 1 g; Carbo 22 g; T Fat <1 g; (Saturated Fat <1 g); 1% Cal from Fat; Chol 0 mg; Fiber <1 g; Sod 4 mg; Calcium 20 mg

Mint Julep

1 lump sugar
7 small sprigs of mint
1¹/2 to 2 ounces (3 to 4 tablespoons) rye whiskey

Place the sugar lump in a glass and crush. Rub 6 of the mint sprigs between your fingers and add to the glass. Pour in enough whiskey to cover the sugar and mint. Let stand for 10 minutes. Fill the glass with finely crushed ice and stir. Garnish with the remaining sprig of mint.

Serves 1

Nutrients Per Serving: Cal 141; Prot 0 g; Carbo 3 g; T Fat 0 g; (Saturated Fat 0 g); 0% Cal from Fat; Chol 0 mg; Fiber 0 g; Sod 1 mg; Calcium <1 mg

Soups
Salads &
Breads

Soups Salads & Breads

Bean and Kale Soup

4 to 8 large garlic cloves, minced
1 tablespoon olive oil
6 cups drained cooked cannellini
4 to 5 cups vegetable or chicken broth
2 tablespoons (rounded) tomato paste
$1/2$ teaspoon sage
1 teaspoon salt
8 ounces kale, trimmed, chopped (4 cups chopped)
Juice of 1 lemon
Freshly grated Parmesan cheese to taste

Sauté the garlic in the olive oil in a stockpot for 30 seconds. Stir in 3 cups of the beans and some of the broth.

Process the remaining 3 cups beans and remaining broth in a blender until puréed. Add the tomato paste and sage. Process until blended. Add the purée to the stockpot and mix well. Stir in the salt. Add the kale and mix well.

Bring the soup to a boil; reduce the heat. Simmer for 30 minutes or until the kale is tender, stirring occasionally. Stir in the lemon juice just before serving. Ladle into soup bowls. Top each serving with cheese.

Serves 6

Nutrients Per Serving: Cal 270; Prot 14 g; Carbo 46 g; T Fat 4 g; (Saturated Fat <1 g); 14% Cal from Fat; Chol 0 mg; Fiber 11 g; Sod 1832 mg; Calcium 143 mg

A primer on dried beans and lentils: Cannellini are white Italian kidney beans, good with tomato dishes. Kidney beans are reddish-brown in color and used in chili and Mexican dishes. Pinto beans are similar to kidney beans but freckled. Black beans are black in color and the staple of South American soups.

Chicken and Pasta Soup

Will chicken soup really speed recovery from the common cold? Maybe so, or perhaps the hot chicken soup is comfort food. Maybe it's the warming effect spread throughout the body, or maybe it's the warmth that helps open the nasal passages. Whatever the reason, many people believe it works. Relax and enjoy!

4 cups chicken or turkey stock
2 cups chopped cooked chicken or turkey
1 medium onion, sliced
2 ribs celery, chopped
1 medium carrot, chopped
4 ounces shell pasta
Salt and pepper to taste
1 (12-ounce) can evaporated milk

Combine the stock, chicken, onion, celery and carrot in a large saucepan and mix well. Bring to a boil; reduce the heat. Simmer for 15 to 20 minutes, stirring occasionally. Stir in the pasta.

Simmer until the pasta is tender, stirring occasionally. Season with salt and pepper. Stir in the evaporated milk just before serving. Ladle into soup bowls.

Serves 8

Nutrients Per Serving: Cal 181; Prot 14 g; Carbo 17 g; T Fat 6 g; (Saturated Fat 3 g); 29% Cal from Fat; Chol 41 mg; Fiber 1 g; Sod 424 mg; Calcium 133 mg

Corn Chowder

1 medium onion, chopped
1 to 2 tablespoons olive oil
1 cup chopped celery
5 medium potatoes, peeled, coarsely chopped
2 cups water
2 low-sodium chicken bouillon cubes
1 quart 1% milk
1 (17-ounce) can whole kernel corn, drained
1 (17-ounce) can cream-style corn
Pepper to taste

Sauté the onion in the olive oil in a stockpot for 1 minute. Stir in the celery. Sauté for 1 minute. Add the potatoes, water and bouillon cubes and mix well.

Cook until the potatoes are tender, stirring occasionally. Stir in the 1% milk, whole kernel corn and cream-style corn. Simmer until heated through, stirring occasionally; do not boil. Season with pepper. Ladle into soup bowls.

Makes 8 (1-cup) servings

Nutrients Per Serving: Cal 289; Prot 10 g; Carbo 54 g; T Fat 6 g; (Saturated Fat 1 g); 17% Cal from Fat; Chol 5 mg; Fiber 5 g; Sod 385 mg; Calcium 173 mg

Corn contributes to a healthy diet with an abundant supply of vitamin C, potassium, magnesium, and fiber.

Maryland Crab Chowder

2 medium onions, chopped
4 ribs celery, chopped
6 small carrots, chopped
7 garlic cloves, minced
2 tablespoons olive oil
8 cups water
8 small new potatoes, peeled, chopped
3 tablespoons chicken base
2 (28-ounce) cans diced tomatoes
1 (6-ounce) can tomato paste
2 1/2 tablespoons Old Bay seasoning
2 pounds fresh crab meat, drained, shells and cartilage removed, flaked

Sauté the onions, celery, carrots and garlic in the olive oil in a stockpot until the vegetables are tender. Stir in the water, potatoes and chicken base. Bring to a boil; reduce the heat.

Simmer, covered, for 30 minutes, stirring occasionally. Add the undrained tomatoes, tomato paste and Old Bay seasoning and mix well. Bring to a boil; reduce the heat. Simmer for 30 minutes, stirring occasionally. Stir in the crab meat. Simmer just until heated through. Ladle into soup bowls.

Makes 12 (1-cup) servings

Nutrients Per Serving: Cal 185; Prot 6 g; Carbo 36 g; T Fat 3 g; (Saturated Fat <1 g);
14% Cal from Fat; Chol 4 mg; Fiber 6 g; Sod 1614 mg; Calcium 57 mg

Old-Fashioned Crab Soup

8 cups water
8 slices bacon, cut into 1-inch pieces
1 (28-ounce) can tomato purée
1¹/₂ pounds cabbage, chopped
1¹/₂ pounds potatoes, chopped
1 pound carrots, chopped
1 large green bell pepper, chopped
2 medium onions, chopped
6 ribs celery, chopped
1 (10-ounce) package frozen lima beans
¹/₄ cup barley
1 (17-ounce) can green peas, drained
1 (12-ounce) can Shoe Peg corn, drained
1 tablespoon Old Bay seasoning
2 pounds fresh crab meat, drained, shells and cartilage removed, flaked

Combine the water and bacon in a stockpot. Bring to a boil; reduce the heat. Cook for 20 minutes. Stir in the tomato purée, cabbage, potatoes, carrots, bell pepper, onions, celery, lima beans and barley. Bring to a boil; reduce the heat.

Cook for 30 minutes or until the vegetables are tender, stirring occasionally. Stir in the peas, corn and Old Bay seasoning. Bring to a boil. Stir in the crab meat. Cook until heated through, stirring occasionally. Ladle into soup bowls.

Makes 20 (1¹/₂-cup) servings

Nutrients Per Serving: Cal 175; Prot 6 g; Carbo 27 g; T Fat 6 g; (Saturated Fat 2 g); 28% Cal from Fat; Chol 7 mg; Fiber 6 g; Sod 467 mg; Calcium 52 mg

Summertime in Maryland is full of seafood festivals and even crab feast cruises at the Inner Harbor in Baltimore. This recipe has been a favorite for over twenty years at the Seafood Feast-i-val held every August at Sailwinds Park in Cambridge.

Oyster Stew

1 pint oysters with liquor
1 quart milk
1/4 cup (1/2 stick) butter or margarine
1/2 teaspoon seafood seasoning (optional)
Salt and pepper to taste

Heat the undrained oysters in a large saucepan over medium heat until the edges just begin to curl. Add the milk, butter and seafood seasoning and mix well.

Simmer until heated through, stirring occasionally; do not boil. Season with salt and pepper. Ladle into soup bowls. Serve immediately.

Makes 6 (1-cup) servings

Nutrients Per Serving: Cal 225; Prot 11 g; Carbo 11 g; T Fat 15 g; (Saturated Fat 9 g); 61% Cal from Fat; Chol 88 mg; Fiber 0 g; Sod 250 mg; Calcium 233 mg

Oysters, a staple of the diet in the Chesapeake Bay area, can be purchased live in the shell, fresh shucked, frozen, or canned. Shucked oysters come in three grades or sizes: counts, selects, and standards. Counts are the largest; use them in stews and entrées. Selects are smaller; use them for frying or hors d'oeuvre. Standards are the smallest and are often used to make oyster fritters.

Lentil and Barley Soup

3/4 cup dried lentils
3/4 cup chopped onion
3/4 cup chopped celery
1 garlic clove, minced
2 tablespoons olive oil
7 cups water
1 (28-ounce) can whole tomatoes, chopped
3/4 cup barley
1 teaspoon salt
1/2 teaspoon oregano, crushed
1 cup thinly sliced carrots

Sort and rinse the lentils. Sauté the onion, celery and garlic in the olive oil in a stockpot until the vegetables are tender. Stir in the lentils, water, undrained tomatoes, barley, salt and oregano. Bring to a boil; reduce the heat.

Simmer, covered, for 30 minutes, stirring occasionally and adding additional water if needed for a thinner consistency. Add the carrots and mix well. Cook for 30 minutes longer or until the carrots are tender, stirring occasionally. Ladle into soup bowls.

Serves 8

Nutrients Per Serving: Cal 184; Prot 7 g; Carbo 32 g; T Fat 4 g; (Saturated Fat 1 g); 19% Cal from Fat; Chol 0 mg; Fiber 9 g; Sod 456 mg; Calcium 57 mg

This soup makes a nice winter meal. Try serving with assorted breads, fresh fruits, and cheese. Lentils and barley both contain soluble fiber, which can help to lower blood cholesterol and/or blood sugar levels.

Lentil Soup with Ham

1 pound dried lentils
1 cup chopped carrots
1 cup chopped onion
1 cup chopped celery
2 garlic cloves, minced
1 tablespoon olive oil
6 cups ham or chicken stock
1 cup chopped cooked ham or turkey ham
1 tablespoon tomato paste
1/2 teaspoon thyme
1 bay leaf
Pepper to taste

Sort and rinse the lentils. Sauté the carrots, onion, celery and garlic in the olive oil in a stockpot until the vegetables are tender. Add the lentils, stock, ham, tomato paste, thyme, bay leaf and pepper and mix well. Bring to a boil; reduce the heat.

Simmer, covered, until the lentils are tender, stirring occasionally. Discard the bay leaf. Ladle into soup bowls. For a thicker consistency, remove 1 to 2 cups of the lentil mixture and mash. Add the mashed mixture to the remaining soup and heat just until warm.

Serves 8

Nutrients Per Serving: Cal 248; Prot 20 g; Carbo 35 g; T Fat 4 g; (Saturated Fat 1 g); 14% Cal from Fat; Chol 17 mg; Fiber 13 g; Sod 405 mg; Calcium 50 mg

There is nothing better than a delicious bowl of warm soup on a cold day. Complete this meal with a colorful green salad and fresh fruit for dessert.

German Lentil Soup

1 pound dried lentils
4 slices bacon, chopped
3 medium onions, sliced
4 medium carrots, sliced
1 cup sliced celery
8 cups hot water
1 ham bone
2 teaspoons basil
2 teaspoons salt

1 teaspoon thyme
1/2 teaspoon black pepper
1/2 teaspoon ginger
1/4 teaspoon celery seeds
1/8 teaspoon cayenne pepper
2 bay leaves
2 tablespoons lemon juice
Salt to taste

German immigrants have had a strong influence on Maryland's cuisine, including this lentil soup recipe. Curious about your ancestors? Visit the Maryland State Archives in Annapolis, where there is a public searchroom for family history and historical research.

Sort and rinse the lentils. Fry the bacon in a stockpot until light brown; push the bacon to the side of the stockpot. Add the onions, carrots and celery to the stockpot. Cook over medium heat for 5 minutes or until the onions are tender, stirring frequently. Add the lentils, hot water, ham bone, basil, 2 teaspoons salt, thyme, black pepper, ginger, celery seeds, cayenne pepper and bay leaves.

Simmer, covered, over low heat for 1 hour or until the lentils are tender, stirring occasionally. Discard the bay leaves. Remove the ham bone to a cutting board. Cut any remaining meat from the bone into bite-size pieces. Return the ham to the stockpot, discarding the bone. Stir in the lemon juice and season with salt to taste. Ladle into soup bowls.

Makes 11 (1-cup) servings

Nutrients Per Serving: Cal 209; Prot 12 g; Carbo 27 g; T Fat 6 g; (Saturated Fat 3 g); 26% Cal from Fat; Chol 11 mg; Fiber 10 g; Sod 504 mg; Calcium 39 mg

Gazpacho (Andalusian Cold Soup)

6 medium tomatoes, peeled, minced
2 medium cucumbers, seeded, minced
1 medium onion, minced
1 (4-ounce) jar pimientos, drained, minced
1 large garlic clove, minced
1 1/2 cups tomato juice
5 tablespoons dry red wine
1/4 cup olive oil
1 tablespoon salt
1 teaspoon paprika
1/4 teaspoon black pepper
1/8 teaspoon cayenne pepper
Minced fresh parsley to taste

Combine the tomatoes, cucumbers, onion, pimientos and garlic in a large glass bowl and mix well. Stir in the tomato juice, wine, olive oil, salt, paprika, black pepper and cayenne pepper. Chill, covered, for several hours. Ladle into soup bowls. Sprinkle with parsley.

Makes 8 (1-cup) servings

Nutrients Per Serving: Cal 114; Prot 2 g; Carbo 11 g; T Fat 7 g; (Saturated Fat 1 g); 53% Cal from Fat; Chol 0 mg; Fiber 2 g; Sod 1048 mg; Calcium 30 mg

Zucchini Soup

3 cups chopped zucchini
2 medium onions, chopped
1 tablespoon olive oil
6 cups chicken broth

1 (10-ounce) package frozen
    lima beans
1/2 (10-ounce) package frozen
    peas
Salt and pepper to taste

Sauté the zucchini and onions in the olive oil in a large saucepan for about 10 minutes. Stir in the broth. Bring to a boil. Stir in the lima beans and peas. Reduce the heat. Simmer for 25 minutes, stirring occasionally. Process the soup in a blender or food processor in batches until puréed. Return the purée to the saucepan. Season with salt and pepper. Simmer just until heated through, stirring frequently. Ladle into soup bowls.

Serves 8

Nutrients Per Serving: Cal 122; Prot 8 g; Carbo 16 g; T Fat 3 g; (Saturated Fat 1 g); 22% Cal from Fat; Chol 0 mg; Fiber 4 g; Sod 622 mg; Calcium 36 mg

Vegetable Soup

2 pounds beef stew meat
Salt to taste
2 cups frozen lima beans
2 cups frozen corn
2 cups frozen green beans
1 (15-ounce) can tomato sauce

1 (14-ounce) can stewed
    tomatoes
1 onion, chopped
3 ribs celery, chopped
3 or 4 carrots, sliced
6 medium potatoes, chopped

Combine the stew meat and salt with a generous amount of water in a large saucepan. Bring to a boil; reduce the heat. Simmer for 1 hour. Strain, reserving the stock and discarding the beef. Combine the reserved stock and the next 8 ingredients in a stockpot. Bring to a boil; reduce the heat. Cook for 40 minutes, stirring occasionally. Stir in the potatoes. Cook for 20 minutes longer, stirring occasionally. Ladle into soup bowls.

Serves 10

Nutrients Per Serving: Cal 301; Prot 24 g; Carbo 40 g; T Fat 7 g; (Saturated Fat 2 g); 19% Cal from Fat; Chol 56 mg; Fiber 7 g; Sod 450 mg; Calcium 71 mg
Nutritional profile includes all of the ingredients.

Apricot Dream Salad

1 (8-ounce) can crushed pineapple
1 (3-ounce) package apricot gelatin
1/2 cup sugar
1/2 cup water
6 ounces cream cheese, softened
1 1/2 cups frozen whipped topping, thawed
1/2 cup chopped pecans

Combine the undrained pineapple, gelatin, sugar and water in a saucepan and mix well. Cook over medium heat for 10 minutes, stirring frequently. Reduce the heat. Add the cream cheese.

Cook until the cream cheese melts and the mixture is smooth, stirring frequently. Chill until set. Fold in the whipped topping and pecans. Spoon the gelatin mixture into an 8×8-inch dish. Chill, covered, until set.

Makes 16 (2-inch) squares

Nutrients Per Serving: Cal 136; Prot 2 g; Carbo 16 g; T Fat 8 g; (Saturated Fat 4 g); 49% Cal from Fat; Chol 12 mg; Fiber <1 g; Sod 44 mg; Calcium 13 mg

Save calories by using sugar-free gelatin, nonfat cream cheese, and reduced-fat whipped topping.

Roasted Asparagus and Parmesan Salad

2 1/4 pounds fresh asparagus
3 tablespoons olive oil
1/2 teaspoon salt
Freshly ground pepper to taste
3 ounces Parmesan cheese, grated
Fresh lemon juice (optional)

Snap off the woody ends of the asparagus spears and peel as needed. Place the trimmed asparagus spears in a large bowl. Drizzle with a mixture of the olive oil and salt. Sprinkle with pepper and turn to coat. Let stand for 10 minutes, turning occasionally.

Arrange the asparagus in a single layer on baking sheets. Roast at 500 degrees for 10 to 12 minutes, shaking the baking sheets several times to prevent the asparagus from sticking. Return the asparagus to the same bowl and turn to coat with any remaining olive oil mixture. Let stand for 5 minutes. Sprinkle with the cheese. Drizzle with lemon juice or additional olive oil if desired.

Serves 6

Nutrients Per Serving: Cal 170; Prot 10 g; Carbo 8 g; T Fat 11 g; (Saturated Fat 4 g); 59% Cal from Fat; Chol 11 mg; Fiber 4 g; Sod 458 mg; Calcium 232 mg

Did you know that asparagus contains about one-third of the recommended daily amount of folic acid, a B vitamin that has been shown in recent years to minimize birth defects? It is also a fairly good source of vitamin C and potassium.

Black Bean Salad

Hot peppers may not only heat up your mouth, but if improperly handled they can also cause painful burning to your face and eyes. To keep the heat where it belongs follow these simple guidelines: wear gloves when peeling, seeding, or chopping peppers; remember never to touch your face or eyes until you have washed your hands thoroughly with warm soapy water; and do not touch your children or pets until you have washed your hands.

4 (16-ounce) cans black beans, rinsed, drained
1 or 2 assorted bell peppers (green, yellow or red), chopped
6 to 8 ounces frozen corn
2 to 3 tablespoons minced jalapeño chiles
1/4 cup chopped fresh cilantro
3 tablespoons minced red onion
2 to 3 teaspoons minced garlic
1/3 cup peanut oil
1/4 cup fresh lime juice
2 tablespoons red wine vinegar
1 tablespoon sugar

Combine the beans, bell peppers, corn, jalapeño chiles, 1/2 of the cilantro, 1/2 of the onion and 1/2 of the garlic in a bowl and mix gently. Combine the peanut oil, lime juice, vinegar, sugar, remaining cilantro, remaining onion and remaining garlic in a bowl and mix well. Pour the peanut oil mixture over the bean mixture and toss to coat.

Marinate, covered, in the refrigerator for 2 to 10 hours, stirring occasionally. Add an additional 2 tablespoons chopped fresh cilantro before serving if desired.

Serves 10

Nutrients Per Serving: Cal 244; Prot 10 g; Carbo 35 g; T Fat 7 g; (Saturated Fat 1 g); 27% Cal from Fat; Chol 0 mg; Fiber 8 g; Sod 573 mg; Calcium 63 mg

Mexican Bean Salad

1 (15-ounce) can black-eyed peas, rinsed, drained
1 (15-ounce) can black beans, rinsed, drained
1 (15-ounce) can dark kidney beans, rinsed, drained
1 (8-ounce) can whole kernel corn, rinsed, drained
1 (2-ounce) jar diced pimento, drained
2 medium carrots, peeled, chopped
1/2 cup cider vinegar
1/3 cup olive oil
1/2 teaspoon chili powder
1/2 teaspoon pepper
1/2 teaspoon salt
1/8 teaspoon garlic powder

Combine the peas, black beans and kidney beans in a 1 1/2- or 2-quart plastic container. Stir in the corn, pimento and carrots.

Whisk the vinegar, olive oil, chili powder, pepper, salt and garlic powder in a bowl. Add the olive oil mixture to the bean mixture and mix well. Chill, tightly covered, for 8 to 10 hours to allow the flavors to marry, stirring occasionally. Stir before serving.

Makes 16 (1/3-cup) servings

Nutrients Per Serving: Cal 120; Prot 5 g; Carbo 15 g; T Fat 5 g; (Saturated Fat 1 g); 34% Cal from Fat; Chol 0 mg; Fiber 4 g; Sod 315 mg; Calcium 33 mg

Black Bean and Rice Salad

1 (15-ounce) can black beans, rinsed, drained
1 cup instant brown rice, prepared
1 red bell pepper, julienned
2 green onions, sliced
2 tablespoons chopped fresh cilantro or parsley
1 teaspoon cumin
1/2 cup reduced-fat peppercorn ranch salad dressing

    Combine the beans, rice, bell pepper, green onions, cilantro and cumin in a bowl and mix well. Add the dressing and toss to coat. Chill, covered, for 8 to 10 hours, stirring once or twice. Spoon the salad onto lettuce-lined salad plates.

Serves 4

Nutrients Per Serving: Cal 229; Prot 8 g; Carbo 39 g; T Fat 4 g; (Saturated Fat 1 g); 15% Cal from Fat; Chol 5 mg; Fiber 6 g; Sod 562 mg; Calcium 62 mg

Use Canadian bacon, low-fat Cheddar cheese, and fat-free mayonnaise-type salad dressing in Colorful Broccoli Salad for a more heart-healthy salad.

Colorful Broccoli Salad

Florets of 3 bunches broccoli
1 cup golden raisins
1 cup (4 ounces) shredded sharp Cheddar cheese
1 cup chopped walnuts
1 (3-ounce) jar bacon bits
1 small red onion, finely chopped
1 cup mayonnaise
1/4 cup sugar
3 tablespoons vinegar

    Combine the broccoli, raisins, cheese, walnuts, bacon bits and onion in a bowl and mix well. Mix the mayonnaise, sugar and vinegar in a bowl. Add the mayonnaise mixture to the broccoli mixture and stir until coated. Chill, covered, for 8 to 10 hours. Serve chilled.

Makes 12 (1/2-cup) servings

Nutrients Per Serving: Cal 338; Prot 9 g; Carbo 20 g; T Fat 26 g; (Saturated Fat 6 g); 66% Cal from Fat; Chol 28 mg; Fiber 3 g; Sod 408 mg; Calcium 125 mg

Chiapparelli's Salad

1 1/2 cups (6 ounces) grated Parmesan cheese
1/2 onion, thinly sliced
2 hard-cooked eggs, finely chopped
1 cup olive oil
1/2 cup red wine vinegar
1 tablespoon oregano
1 tablespoon salt
1 garlic clove, crushed
1/8 teaspoon pepper
1/8 teaspoon sugar
2 or 3 heads lettuce, trimmed, torn

Toss the cheese, onion and eggs in a large salad bowl. Whisk the olive oil, vinegar, oregano, salt, garlic, pepper and sugar in a bowl. Add the dressing to the cheese mixture and mix gently. Add the lettuce just before serving and toss to coat.

Serves 15

Nutrients Per Serving: Cal 197; Prot 5 g; Carbo 5 g; T Fat 18 g; (Saturated Fat 4 g); 79% Cal from Fat; Chol 35 mg; Fiber 1 g; Sod 635 mg; Calcium 140 mg

Chiapparelli's restaurant, located in the heart of Little Italy in Baltimore, is an old neighborhood favorite featuring southern Italian classics and their famous house salad.

Italian Salad

Croutons
4 cups cubed dry French bread
1/2 cup (2 ounces) grated Parmesan cheese
1/4 to 1/2 cup vegetable oil
1 teaspoon garlic powder

Italian Dressing
1/2 cup olive oil
1/3 cup red wine vinegar
2 tablespoons ketchup
1 garlic clove, minced
3/4 teaspoon oregano
Salt and cracked pepper to taste

Salad
1 head each romaine, red leaf lettuce and iceberg lettuce, trimmed, torn
1 tablespoon each chopped fresh basil and chopped fresh parsley
1 medium purple onion, sliced
1 pint cherry tomatoes, cut into halves
8 ounces provolone cheese, cubed
3 ounces sliced Genoa salami
1 (6-ounce) can pitted black olives, drained, cut into halves

For the croutons, toss the bread cubes, cheese, oil and garlic powder in a bowl. Spread the bread cubes in a single layer on a baking sheet. Toast at 350 degrees for 20 to 25 minutes or until brown and crisp. Let stand until cool.

For the dressing, combine the olive oil, vinegar, ketchup, garlic, oregano, salt and cracked pepper in a jar with a tight-fitting lid and seal tightly. Shake to mix.

For the salad, toss the romaine, red leaf lettuce, iceberg lettuce, basil and parsley in a salad bowl. Add the onion, cherry tomatoes, cheese, salami and olives and mix well. Add the croutons and dressing and toss to mix.

Serves 12

Nutrients Per Serving: Cal 338; Prot 10 g; Carbo 12 g; T Fat 29 g; (Saturated Fat 7 g); 74% Cal from Fat; Chol 23 mg; Fiber 3 g; Sod 587 mg; Calcium 240 mg

Spinach and Strawberry Salad with Raspberry Dressing

Raspberry Dressing
1/3 cup raspberry vinegar
1/4 cup sugar (optional)
2 tablespoons (rounded) all-fruit raspberry jam or spread
1 1/2 teaspoons grated onion
1 teaspoon dry mustard
1 teaspoon salt

Salad
1 1/2 to 2 (10-ounce) packages baby spinach
1 pint fresh strawberries, sliced
1/2 to 3/4 cup sliced almonds

For the dressing, combine the vinegar, sugar, jam, onion, dry mustard and salt in a blender. Process until smooth.

For the salad, mix the spinach, strawberries and almonds in a salad bowl. Add the dressing and toss to coat.

Serves 8

Nutrients Per Serving: Cal 102; Prot 4 g; Carbo 12 g; T Fat 5 g; (Saturated Fat <1 g); 40% Cal from Fat; Chol 0 mg; Fiber 4 g; Sod 349 mg; Calcium 101 mg

In June, visit farmers' markets and roadside stands to purchase and sample the freshest berries. Call the Maryland Office of Tourism Development at (410) 767-3400, or visit their website (www.mdisfun.org) for a calendar of events including strawberry festivals.

Grilled Cajun Chicken Salad

Cider vinegar and distilled vinegar are two types of white vinegar. White wine vinegar is used often in cooking, and rice wine vinegar is one of the softest and most pleasant. Why not make your own fruit-flavored vinegar? Add preserves or jam to a bottle of red or white wine vinegar and let the vinegar stand at room temperature for a few days. Use the homemade version to create your favorite salad dressings.

Spiced Pecans
1 tablespoon butter
1 teaspoon sugar
1/8 to 1/4 teaspoon cayenne
   pepper
1/2 cup pecan or walnut halves
   or pieces

Mustard Vinaigrette
1/3 cup vegetable oil
3 tablespoons coarse-ground
   mustard
2 tablespoons cider vinegar
1 tablespoon honey
1/8 teaspoon cayenne pepper

Salad
8 ounces boneless skinless
   chicken breasts
1/2 to 1 teaspoon Cajun or
   Creole seasoning
6 cups torn mixed salad greens
1/2 cup red bell pepper strips
1 large tomato, cut into wedges
Sliced mushrooms (optional)
Chopped onion (optional)

For the pecans, heat the butter in a small skillet. Stir in the sugar and cayenne pepper. Add the pecans and mix well. Cook over medium heat for 4 to 5 minutes or until the pecans are lightly toasted, stirring constantly. Let stand until cool.

For the vinaigrette, combine the ingredients in a jar with a tight-fitting lid and seal tightly. Shake to mix. Chill until serving time.

For the salad, sprinkle both sides of the chicken with the Cajun seasoning. Grill, broil or bake the chicken until cooked through. Let stand until cool. Slice the chicken into thin strips. Toss the pecans, chicken, salad greens, bell pepper, tomato, mushrooms and onion in a salad bowl. Add the vinaigrette and toss to coat.

Serves 4

Nutrients Per Serving: Cal 418; Prot 15 g; Carbo 16 g; T Fat 34 g; (Saturated Fat 5 g); 71% Cal from Fat; Chol 39 mg; Fiber 5 g; Sod 379 mg; Calcium 80 mg

Chinese Chicken and Pasta Salad

8 ounces spaghetti
1 cup ultra low-fat mayonnaise-type salad dressing
2 tablespoons soy sauce
1 teaspoon ginger
1/4 teaspoon hot pepper sauce (optional)
2 cups chopped cooked chicken
1 cup chopped red bell pepper
1 cup snow peas
1/4 cup sliced green onions
Freshly ground pepper to taste
Romaine leaves

Cook the pasta using package directions until al dente; drain. Let stand until cool. Combine the salad dressing, soy sauce, ginger and hot pepper sauce in a bowl and mix well. Stir in the pasta, chicken, bell pepper, snow peas and green onions. Season with freshly ground pepper.

Chill, covered, until serving time. Spoon the salad onto romaine-lined salad plates. You may substitute any type of pasta for the spaghetti.

Serves 6

Nutrients Per Serving: Cal 333; Prot 18 g; Carbo 38 g; T Fat 12 g; (Saturated Fat 2 g); 32% Cal from Fat; Chol 46 mg; Fiber 2 g; Sod 828 mg; Calcium 25 mg
Nutritional profile reflects the substitution of lite mayonnaise-type salad dressing for the ultra low-fat mayonnaise-type salad dressing.

Take control of home food safety. Refrigerate foods quickly and at proper temperatures to slow the growth of bacteria and to prevent foodborne illness. Leftover foods should not remain at room temperature more than two hours. In hot weather, 80° F or above, this time is reduced to one hour.

Tomato and Pasta Salad

3 cups shell pasta
1 (14-ounce) can diced tomatoes, drained
1 (2-ounce) can sliced black olives, drained
1/4 cup sliced green onions
1/4 cup each chopped green and yellow bell pepper
1/4 cup thinly sliced carrots
1/2 cup Italian salad dressing
2 tablespoons grated Parmesan cheese (optional)

Cook the pasta using package directions until al dente; drain and rinse with cold water. Combine the pasta, tomatoes, olives, green onions, bell peppers and carrots in a large bowl and mix well. Add the salad dressing and toss to coat. Sprinkle with the cheese.

Serves 6

Nutrients Per Serving: Cal 323; Prot 8 g; Carbo 48 g; T Fat 12 g; (Saturated Fat 2 g); 32% Cal from Fat; Chol 0 mg; Fiber 4 g; Sod 326 mg; Calcium 38 mg

Spinach Tortellini Salad

16 ounces fresh cheese tortellini
5 cups fresh spinach leaves, torn
1 cup coarsely shredded red cabbage
6 slices bacon, crisp-cooked, drained, crumbled
4 green onions, chopped
1/3 cup red wine vinegar and oil salad dressing
1/4 cup chutney

Cook the pasta using package directions; drain. Let stand until cool. Toss the tortellini, spinach, cabbage, bacon and green onions in a salad bowl. Chill, covered, until serving time.

Combine the salad dressing and chutney in a bowl and mix well. Add the chutney mixture to the pasta mixture just before serving and toss to mix. Serve with crusty garlic bread.

Serves 8

Nutrients Per Serving: Cal 205; Prot 9 g; Carbo 24 g; T Fat 9 g; (Saturated Fat 3 g); 38% Cal from Fat; Chol 13 mg; Fiber 3 g; Sod 455 mg; Calcium 116 mg

Nutritious and colorful! Did you know fruits and vegetables that are dark yellow and deep orange in color are high in beta carotene? This chemical turns into vitamin A in your body and helps promote healthy eyesight. Mom was right about eating those carrots.

Maryland Beaten Biscuits

1 cup flour
1/4 cup shortening
1/4 teaspoon salt
1/4 teaspoon baking soda
1/4 teaspoon sugar
1/2 to 3/4 cup water

Combine the flour, shortening, salt, baking soda and sugar in a food processor. Add the water gradually, processing constantly until the mixture adheres and forms a ball.

Divide the dough into 6 equal portions. Process each portion individually in a food processor for 1 minute longer. Combine the 6 portions and knead on a lightly floured surface until smooth. Shape the dough into 1-inch balls and arrange on a lightly buttered baking sheet.

Flatten each ball slightly with a fork and prick 2 or 3 times. Bake at 400 degrees for 20 minutes or until golden brown. Serve warm. You may reheat leftovers.

Makes 6 biscuits

Nutrients Per Serving: Cal 152; Prot 2 g; Carbo 16 g; T Fat 9 g; (Saturated Fat 2 g); 52% Cal from Fat; Chol 0 mg; Fiber 1 g; Sod 150 mg; Calcium 3 mg

"I recommend three Maryland beaten biscuits, with water, for your breakfast," wrote John Barth in The Floating Opera. *"They are as hard as a haulseiner's conscience and dray as a dredger's tongue, and they sit for hours in your morning stomach like ballast on a tender ship's keel."* The Indians taught the early settlers how to make these biscuits known then for their portability and their "staying power." Today's cooking techniques produce a more tender product! Serve them with jam for breakfast or make a tray of "ham biscuits" for brunch.

Sweet Potato Biscuits

2 cups cake flour
1 1/4 cups all-purpose flour
3 tablespoons baking powder
1/2 teaspoon baking soda
3 1/2 cups mashed cooked sweet potatoes
1 1/2 cups sugar
1 1/4 cups (2 1/2 sticks) margarine, softened

Mix the cake flour, all-purpose flour, baking powder and baking soda in a bowl.

Combine the sweet potatoes, sugar and margarine in a mixing bowl. Beat at low speed until blended, scraping the bowl occasionally. Add the flour mixture and beat until well mixed.

Knead the dough in the bowl until smooth. Chill, covered, until firm and cold. Roll the dough 1/4 inch thick on a lightly floured surface. Cut with a round biscuit cutter. Arrange the rounds on a baking sheet sprayed with nonstick cooking spray. Bake at 350 degrees for 15 to 18 minutes or until light brown. Serve warm.

Makes 2 dozen biscuits

Nutrients Per Serving: Cal 249; Prot 3 g; Carbo 39 g; T Fat 10 g; (Saturated Fat 2 g); 35% Cal from Fat; Chol 0 mg; Fiber 1 g; Sod 327 mg; Calcium 118 mg

Successful bread making requires the use of fresh ingredients. Be sure to check the expiration date on baking powder. Don't jeopardize the quality of your product by using ingredients that have expired.

Eastern Shore Corn Bread

1½ cups yellow cornmeal
1 cup flour
¼ cup sugar
2¼ teaspoons baking powder

⅛ teaspoon salt
1 cup milk
2 eggs, beaten
¼ cup vegetable oil

Combine the cornmeal, flour, sugar, baking powder and salt in a bowl and mix well. Stir in the milk, eggs and oil. Spoon the cornmeal mixture into a greased 8x8-inch or 9x9-inch baking pan. Bake at 400 degrees for 25 to 30 minutes or until light brown. Add additional milk for a thinner batter if desired.

Serves 9

Nutrients Per Serving: Cal 233; Prot 5 g; Carbo 34 g; T Fat 9 g; (Saturated Fat 2 g); 34% Cal from Fat; Chol 51 mg; Fiber 2 g; Sod 189 mg; Calcium 109 mg

Banana Bread

¼ cup milk
1 teaspoon vinegar
2 cups flour
1 teaspoon baking soda
½ teaspoon salt

½ cup (1 stick) butter, softened
½ cup sugar
1¼ cups mashed bananas
2 eggs, beaten

Mix the milk and vinegar in a small bowl. Combine the flour, baking soda and salt in a bowl and mix well. Beat the butter and sugar in a mixing bowl until creamy, scraping the bowl occasionally. Add the bananas and eggs and beat until smooth.

Add the dry ingredients and sour milk gradually to the creamed mixture, beating constantly until blended. Spoon the batter into a greased 5x9-inch loaf pan. Bake at 325 degrees for 1 hour. Cool in pan for 10 minutes. Remove to a wire rack to cool completely.

Serves 12

Nutrients Per Serving: Cal 213; Prot 4 g; Carbo 30 g; T Fat 9 g; (Saturated Fat 5 g); 37% Cal from Fat; Chol 57 mg; Fiber 1 g; Sod 294 mg; Calcium 17 mg

Serve Zucchini Soup (page 39) with Surprise Muffins. To prepare the muffins, mix 1 package lite bran muffin mix using package directions. Spoon half the batter into muffin cups sprayed with nonstick cooking spray. Top the batter in each muffin cup with 1 tablespoon of your favorite preserves. Spoon the remaining batter over the preserves. Bake using package directions.

Banana Blueberry Bread

3 cups flour
1 1/3 cups sugar
4 teaspoons baking powder
1 teaspoon salt
1 1/2 cups quick-cooking oats

2 cups mashed ripe bananas
2 cups fresh blueberries
2/3 cup vegetable oil
4 eggs, lightly beaten

Grease the bottoms of two 4x8-inch loaf pans. Combine the flour, sugar, baking powder and salt in a bowl and mix well. Stir in the oats. Add the bananas, blueberries, oil and eggs and stir just until moistened. Spoon the batter evenly into the prepared pans. Bake at 350 degrees for 1 hour or until a wooden pick inserted in the center comes out clean. Cool in pans for 10 minutes. Remove to a wire rack to cool completely.

Makes 24 slices

Nutrients Per Serving: Cal 210; Prot 4 g; Carbo 33 g; T Fat 8 g; (Saturated Fat 1 g); 32% Cal from Fat; Chol 35 mg; Fiber 2 g; Sod 190 mg; Calcium 56 mg

Orange Cranberry Bread

2 cups sifted flour
1/2 teaspoon baking soda
1/2 teaspoon salt
1/2 teaspoon baking powder
1 cup sugar
1 egg, beaten

Juice and chopped pulp of
    1 orange
2 tablespoons margarine
Grated zest of 1 orange
1 to 1 1/2 cups fresh cranberries,
    cut into halves

Mix the flour, baking soda, salt and baking powder. Combine the sugar and egg in a bowl and mix well. Place the orange juice, orange pulp and margarine in a measuring cup. Add boiling water to measure 3/4 cup and stir. Add the boiling water mixture to the sugar mixture and mix well. Stir in the orange zest. Add the flour mixture and mix well. Fold in the cranberries. Spoon the batter into a greased 4x8-inch loaf pan. Bake at 350 degrees for 1 hour or until the loaf tests done. Cool in pan for 10 minutes. Remove to a wire rack to cool completely.

Makes 17 (1/2-inch) slices

Nutrients Per Serving: Cal 120; Prot 2 g; Carbo 24 g; T Fat 2 g; (Saturated Fat <1 g); 13% Cal from Fat; Chol 13 mg; Fiber 1 g; Sod 140 mg; Calcium 17 mg

Pumpkin Cranberry Bread

2¹/₄ cups flour
1 tablespoon pumpkin pie spice
1 teaspoon baking soda
¹/₂ teaspoon salt
2 eggs
2 cups sugar
1 cup canned pumpkin
¹/₂ cup vegetable oil
1 cup chopped cranberries

Combine the flour, pumpkin pie spice, baking soda and salt in a bowl and mix well. Beat the eggs in a mixing bowl until smooth. Add the sugar, pumpkin and oil and beat until blended. Add the pumpkin mixture to the flour mixture and stir just until moistened. Fold in the cranberries.

Spoon the batter into 2 greased and floured 4x8-inch loaf pans. Bake at 350 degrees for 1 hour or until a wooden pick inserted in the center comes out clean. Cool in pans for 5 to 10 minutes. Remove to a wire rack to cool completely.

Makes 24 slices

Nutrients Per Serving: Cal 160; Prot 2 g; Carbo 27 g; T Fat 5 g; (Saturated Fat 1 g); 29% Cal from Fat; Chol 18 mg; Fiber 1 g; Sod 107 mg; Calcium 7 mg

Peter, Peter, pumpkin eater had no idea he had ventured onto an abundant source of beta carotene. A mere one-half cup of canned pumpkin has over five times your daily quota of vitamin A, which is essential for night vision and for growth and health of body tissues.

Garden Vegetable Bread

$1/2$ cup warm (70 to 80 degrees) buttermilk
3 tablespoons warm (70 to 80 degrees) water
1 tablespoon vegetable oil
$2/3$ cup shredded zucchini
$1/4$ cup chopped red bell pepper
2 tablespoons chopped green onions
3 tablespoons grated Parmesan cheese
2 tablespoons sugar
1 teaspoon salt
$1/2$ teaspoon lemon pepper seasoning
$1/2$ cup old-fashioned oats
$2^{1/2}$ cups bread flour
$1^{1/2}$ teaspoons dry yeast

Add the buttermilk, water, oil, zucchini, bell pepper, green onions, cheese, sugar, salt, lemon pepper seasoning, oats, bread flour and yeast to the bread machine pan in the order recommended by the manufacturer.

Set the machine on the dough mode. Check the dough after 5 minutes of mixing, adding 1 to 2 tablespoons of water or flour if needed. Shape the dough into a loaf in a greased 5x9-inch loaf pan. Bake at 375 degrees for 20 to 25 minutes or until the loaf tests done.

Makes 12 slices

Nutrients Per Serving: Cal 147; Prot 5 g; Carbo 26 g; T Fat 2 g; (Saturated Fat 1 g); 15% Cal from Fat; Chol 1 mg; Fiber 1 g; Sod 248 mg; Calcium 38 mg

Gardening is a fun summer activity. Gardeners are always seeking new, creative, and tasty recipes for their homegrown vegetables. This is a good way to use garden vegetables to make bread for sandwiches.

Popovers

2 eggs
1 cup 2% milk
1 cup flour
1/2 teaspoon salt

Generously grease 8 muffin cups. Lightly beat the eggs in a bowl with a fork. Add the 2% milk, flour and salt and stir just until smooth; do not overbeat. Fill the prepared muffin cups 3/4 full. Bake at 450 degrees for 20 minutes. Reduce the oven temperature to 350 degrees.

Bake for 20 minutes longer or until golden brown. Remove the popovers from the muffin cups immediately. Serve hot with butter or margarine.

Leftovers may be reheated on an ungreased baking sheet at 350 degrees for about 5 minutes. Or wrap in foil and freeze for future use. To reheat, remove the foil and heat at 350 degrees for 10 minutes.

Makes 8 popovers

Nutrients Per Serving: Cal 91; Prot 4 g; Carbo 14 g; T Fat 2 g; (Saturated Fat 1 g); 20% Cal from Fat; Chol 55 mg; Fiber <1 g; Sod 177 mg; Calcium 46 mg

Serve Popovers with Fruit Butter. To prepare, combine 2 cups pitted prunes, 1 3/4 cups apple juice, 8 dried figs (stems removed), 1 teaspoon vanilla extract and 1 teaspoon grated orange zest in a 2-quart saucepan. Bring to a simmer. Cook over low heat for 30 minutes, stirring frequently. Let stand until cool. Process the prune mixture in a food processor or blender until smooth. Store tightly covered in the refrigerator.

Nut Rolls

Walnut Filling
4 cups ground walnuts
Sugar to taste
2 tablespoons honey
Warm milk to taste

Rolls
2 cakes yeast
$1/2$ cup lukewarm milk
6 cups sifted flour
3 tablespoons sugar
1 teaspoon salt
1 cup sour cream
$1/2$ cup (1 stick) butter, softened
3 eggs, beaten

For the filling, combine the walnuts and sugar in a bowl and mix well. Stir in the honey. Add just enough warm milk to make of a spreading consistency and mix well.

For the rolls, dissolve the yeast in the lukewarm milk in a bowl and mix well. Combine the flour, sugar and salt in a bowl and mix well. Stir in the sour cream, butter and eggs. Add the yeast mixture and mix well. Knead the dough until smooth. Divide the dough into 8 equal portions. Roll each portion into a rectangle on a lightly floured surface. Spread each rectangle with some of the filling. Roll as for a jelly roll.

Arrange the rolls on a greased baking sheet. Let rise for 1 hour or until doubled in bulk. Bake at 350 degrees for 35 to 40 minutes or until light brown. You may brush the rolls with beaten egg or additional milk before baking.

Makes 8 large rolls

Nutrients Per Serving: Cal 815; Prot 19 g; Carbo 83 g; T Fat 47 g; (Saturated Fat 14 g); 51% Cal from Fat; Chol 125 mg; Fiber 5 g; Sod 458 mg; Calcium 118 mg

John Flynn's Irish Scones

1 cup raisins (optional)
1 1/4 cups each bread flour and cake flour
2 tablespoons (heaping) baking powder

1/2 cup shortening
1/4 cup sugar
1 1/4 teaspoons salt
1 egg
1/2 cup milk

Combine the raisins with enough hot water to cover in a bowl. Let stand for 20 minutes; drain. Combine the bread flour, cake flour and baking powder in a bowl and mix well. Combine the shortening, sugar and salt in a bowl and mix until blended. Stir in the egg. Add the flour mixture gradually and stir until a dough forms. Add the milk gradually and mix well. Stir in the raisins. Shape the dough into rounds and arrange on a baking sheet. Bake at 400 degrees for 20 minutes. Remove to a wire rack to cool.

Makes 1 dozen scones

Nutrients Per Serving: Cal 208; Prot 4 g; Carbo 27 g; T Fat 10 g; (Saturated Fat 3 g); 42% Cal from Fat; Chol 19 mg; Fiber 1 g; Sod 497 mg; Calcium 154 mg

Festive Ham Bread

1 (16-ounce) loaf frozen bread dough
4 ounces cooked ham, chopped
1/2 cup raisins

4 ounces bacon, crisp-cooked, drained, crumbled
1/2 cup sliced pimento-stuffed green olives

Thaw the bread dough using package directions. Roll the bread dough into a 1/4 inch thick rectangle on a lightly floured surface. Sprinkle the rectangle evenly with the ham, raisins, bacon and olives. Roll as for a jelly roll to enclose the filling, turning the ends under. Arrange the roll seam side down on a greased baking sheet.

Bake at 350 degrees for 25 to 30 minutes or until light brown. Cut into 6 slices. Serve hot or cold. Store leftovers, wrapped in foil, in the refrigerator.

Makes 6 (2-inch) slices

Nutrients Per Serving: Cal 333; Prot 16 g; Carbo 49 g; T Fat 10 g; (Saturated Fat 2 g); 25% Cal from Fat; Chol 23 mg; Fiber 3 g; Sod 768 mg; Calcium 32 mg

Irish immigrants began arriving in Baltimore in large numbers in 1846. Out of 418,000 Marylanders counted in the 1850 census, 20,000 had been born in Ireland. The Irish settled in Baltimore at Fells Point and Locust Point. They settled in nearby communities such as Cockeysville, Catonsville, Hydes, Harford, and Belair. They gave Irish names to the towns of Dundalk, Dublin, New Market, and Whitehall. Others went west to the coal and railroad towns of Cumberland and Frostburg.

Stromboli-for-a-Crowd

2 (16-ounce) loaves frozen bread dough
1¹/₂ cups (6 ounces) shredded low-fat mozzarella cheese
8 ounces thinly sliced low-fat ham
¹/₂ cup chopped fresh parsley
1 egg
1 teaspoon water
1 (15-ounce) can pizza sauce

Thaw the bread dough using package directions. Line an 11×17-inch baking sheet with foil. Spray the foil lightly with nonstick cooking spray.

Roll 1 bread loaf into a 10×14-inch rectangle on a lightly floured surface. Sprinkle with ¹/₄ cup of the cheese to within ¹/₂ inch of the edges. Top with 2 ounces of the ham, overlapping the slices. Sprinkle with ¹/₄ cup of the cheese and top with 2 ounces of the ham, overlapping the slices. Sprinkle with half the parsley and ¹/₄ cup of the cheese. Roll as for a jelly roll to enclose the filling, sealing the edge and ends. Repeat the process with the remaining bread dough, cheese, ham and parsley.

Arrange the rolls seam side down 4 inches apart on the prepared baking sheet. Make 3 slits in the top of each roll. Whisk the egg and water in a bowl. Brush the tops of the rolls with the egg wash. Bake at 375 degrees for 30 minutes or until golden brown. Cool slightly on baking sheet. Cut into 1-inch slices. Serve warm with the pizza sauce as a topping.

Serves 12

Nutrients Per Serving: Cal 290; Prot 16 g; Carbo 43 g; T Fat 7 g; (Saturated Fat 2 g); 20% Cal from Fat; Chol 36 mg; Fiber 3 g; Sod 863 mg; Calcium 126 mg

Assemble the stromboli and put it into the oven when the Ravens' game begins. It will be ready for halftime! Serve with Chiapparelli's Salad on page 45.

Entrées

Entrées

Teriyaki Steak

1 (2-pound) beef flank steak, 3/4 to 1 inch thick
1/2 cup soy sauce
2 tablespoons brown sugar
2 tablespoons Worcestershire sauce
1 garlic clove, minced
1 tablespoon vinegar
3/4 teaspoon ginger

Place the steak in a shallow glass or plastic dish. Combine the soy sauce, brown sugar, Worcestershire sauce, garlic, vinegar and ginger in a bowl and mix well. Pour the soy sauce mixture over the steak, turning to coat. Marinate, covered, in the refrigerator for 8 to 10 hours, turning occasionally.

Drain the steak 20 minutes before serving, discarding the marinade. Place the steak on a broiler rack in a broiler pan. Broil for 5 minutes per side or until medium rare. Slice diagonally across the grain.

Serves 8

Nutrients Per Serving: Cal 208; Prot 25 g; Carbo 6 g; T Fat 9 g; (Saturated Fat 4 g); 39% Cal from Fat; Chol 59 mg; Fiber <1 g; Sod 1431 mg; Calcium 17 mg
Nutritional profile includes the entire amount of marinade.

Marinate the steak the day before and spend the day sightseeing. Visit historic Fort McHenry in Baltimore, where Francis Scott Key wrote "The Star-Spangled Banner," our national anthem.

Beef with Green Peppers and Tomatoes

12 ounces lean beef flank or
   round steak
2 tablespoons thin reduced-
   sodium soy sauce
2 tablespoons flour
1/4 teaspoon baking soda
1 garlic clove, crushed
1 tablespoon chopped scallions
1 tablespoon fermented black
   beans
1 tablespoon chopped fresh
   gingerroot
1 1/2 teaspoons vegetable oil

1 tablespoon wine
1 1/2 teaspoons vegetable oil
2 cups sliced green bell
   peppers
1/2 cup chicken stock
2 teaspoons cornstarch
1/8 teaspoon pepper
2 tomatoes, each cut into
   6 wedges
1/8 teaspoon sesame oil
2 or 3 scallions, cut into 1-inch
   slices

Cut the steak into 1-inch strips, about 1/8 to 1/4 inch thick. Combine the soy sauce, flour and baking soda in a shallow glass or plastic dish and mix well. Add the steak and toss to coat. Marinate for 30 minutes, stirring 2 or 3 times. Combine the garlic, 1 tablespoon chopped scallions, fermented black beans and gingerroot in a bowl and mix well.

Heat 1 1/2 teaspoons vegetable oil in a wok. Stir the garlic mixture into the hot oil. Stir-fry for 1 minute or until light brown. Add the undrained steak. Stir-fry for 1 minute. Add the wine. Stir-fry for 30 seconds. Remove the steak to a platter.

Add 1 1/2 teaspoons vegetable oil to the hot wok. Add the bell peppers. Stir-fry for 30 seconds. Return the steak to the wok. Stir in a mixture of the stock, cornstarch and pepper. Stir-fry for 30 seconds or until slightly thickened. Add the tomatoes and sesame oil. Stir gently 3 or 4 times. Spoon the stir-fry mixture onto a serving platter. Top with 2 or 3 sliced scallions. Serve with hot cooked white rice.

Serves 4

Nutrients Per Serving: Cal 240; Prot 21 g; Carbo 14 g; T Fat 11 g; (Saturated Fat 3 g); 41% Cal from Fat; Chol 44 mg; Fiber 2 g; Sod 481 mg; Calcium 30 mg

Asian Beef with Savoy Cabbage

1 (1-pound) beef sirloin steak
1/4 cup ultra low-fat Catalina salad dressing
1 small head savoy cabbage, thinly shredded
1 small red onion, thinly sliced
1/2 cup ultra low-fat Catalina salad dressing
3 tablespoons soy sauce
1 tablespoon brown sugar
Crushed red pepper flakes to taste
2 tablespoons sesame seeds, toasted (optional)
2 tablespoons chopped fresh cilantro (optional)

Place the steak in a shallow glass or plastic dish. Brush both sides of the steak with 1/4 cup salad dressing. Marinate, covered with plastic wrap, in the refrigerator for 2 to 10 hours, turning once. Arrange the steak on a rack in a broiler pan. Broil until the desired degree of doneness. Cool slightly. Cut into thin strips.

Toss the cabbage and onion in a salad bowl or arrange on a serving platter. Heat 1/2 cup salad dressing, soy sauce and brown sugar in a saucepan, stirring frequently.

Add the steak and red pepper flakes and mix well. Spoon the steak mixture over the cabbage mixture. Sprinkle with the sesame seeds and cilantro. Serve warm.

Serves 4

Nutrients Per Serving: Cal 265; Prot 27 g; Carbo 19 g; T Fat 9 g; (Saturated Fat 3 g); 30% Cal from Fat; Chol 75 mg; Fiber 1 g; Sod 1437 mg; Calcium 34 mg
Nutritional profile reflects the substitution of lite Catalina salad dressing for the ultra low-fat Catalina salad dressing.

Savoy cabbage is mainly grown in Western Europe but is also found in small amounts in Northern and Eastern Europe, Western Mediterranean areas, and North America. Savoy has a loose, full head of crinkled leaves that vary in color from dark green to pale green. Considered by some as the best cabbage for cooking, it has a mellow flavor. Choose a head that is heavy for its size. Leaves should be crisp, not limp, and there should be no sign of browning. Store in a sealable plastic bag in the refrigerator for up to one week.

Beef Casserole

1 pound lean ground beef
1 cup sliced carrots
1/2 cup chopped celery
2 large potatoes, sliced
1 medium onion, thinly sliced
1 (4-ounce) can mushrooms,
     drained

1 small green bell pepper,
     chopped
1/4 teaspoon basil
1/4 teaspoon tarragon
Pepper to taste
1 (10-ounce) can tomato soup

Layer the ground beef, carrots, celery, potatoes, onion, mushrooms, bell pepper, basil, tarragon, pepper and soup in the order listed in a large deep saucepan or a 9x13-inch baking dish.

For the saucepan, cook, covered, over medium heat for 15 minutes or until the ground beef is brown; stir. Cook, covered, over low heat for 45 minutes longer. For the baking dish, bake, covered with foil, at 350 degrees for 1 hour. Serve with a tossed green salad and crusty French bread.

Serves 4

Nutrients Per Serving: Cal 399; Prot 30 g; Carbo 35 g; T Fat 17 g; (Saturated Fat 6 g); 37% Cal from Fat; Chol 81 mg; Fiber 5 g; Sod 635 mg; Calcium 52 mg

Southern Barbecue Sauce

2 garlic cloves, crushed
2 tablespoons margarine
1 cup ketchup
3/4 cup chili sauce
2 tablespoons prepared
     mustard

1/4 cup packed brown sugar
2 tablespoons Worcestershire
     sauce
1 tablespoon celery seeds
1/2 teaspoon salt
1/8 to 1/4 teaspoon hot sauce

Sauté the garlic in the margarine in a saucepan for 4 to 5 minutes. Stir in the ketchup, chili sauce, prepared mustard, brown sugar, Worcestershire sauce, celery seeds, salt and hot sauce. Bring to a boil, stirring occasionally. Remove from heat. Use to baste approximately 4 pounds of ribs or chicken.

Makes 2 cups

Nutrients Per Serving: Cal 30; Prot <1 g; Carbo 6 g; T Fat 1 g; (Saturated Fat <1 g); 24% Cal from Fat; Chol 0 mg; Fiber <1 g; Sod 244 mg; Calcium 10 mg

Honey Mustard Pork Tenderloin

2 (12-ounce) boneless pork tenderloins, trimmed
1/4 cup honey
2 tablespoons apple cider vinegar
1 tablespoon Dijon mustard
1/2 teaspoon paprika

Spray a broiler rack and broiler pan with nonstick cooking spray. Arrange the tenderloins on the prepared rack and place in the prepared broiler pan. Combine the honey, vinegar, Dijon mustard and paprika in a bowl and mix well.

Spoon 1/3 of the mustard sauce over the tenderloins. Bake at 350 degrees for 30 minutes or until a meat thermometer registers 160 degrees, basting occasionally with the remaining sauce. Slice as desired.

Serves 6

Nutrients Per Serving: Cal 186; Prot 24 g; Carbo 12 g; T Fat 4 g; (Saturated Fat 1 g); 21% Cal from Fat; Chol 67 mg; Fiber <1 g; Sod 111 mg; Calcium 10 mg

Pork can easily be part of a healthy diet. The key is to look for lean varieties and to trim all visible fat. Lean tenderloin derives only twenty-six percent of its calories from fat, a close second to skinless chicken breast, which is twenty percent calories from fat. Center loin, lean ham, and Canadian bacon are also lean pork choices.

Best-Ever Pork Chops

6 (6-ounce) pork loin chops, trimmed
1/2 teaspoon basil
Salt and pepper to taste
1/2 cup white wine
1 (32-ounce) package herb-seasoned stuffing mix
1 cup milk

Arrange the pork chops in a single layer in a baking dish. Sprinkle with the basil, salt and pepper and drizzle with the wine. Top with the stuffing mix. Pour the milk over the prepared layers. Bake, covered, at 350 degrees for 1 hour.

Serves 6

Nutrients Per Serving: Cal 952; Prot 59 g; Carbo 100 g; T Fat 32 g; (Saturated Fat 8 g); 31% Cal from Fat; Chol 123 mg; Fiber 9 g; Sod 1693 mg; Calcium 251 mg

Orange-Glazed Pork Chops

4 (2-ounce) top loin pork chops
1/2 cup orange juice
Salt and pepper to taste
2 tablespoons brown sugar

2 tablespoons orange
   marmalade
1 tablespoon vinegar

Brown the pork chops on both sides in a skillet sprayed with nonstick cooking spray, adding orange juice as needed to prevent the chops from overbrowning. Season with salt and pepper. Combine the remaining orange juice, brown sugar, marmalade and vinegar in a bowl and mix well. Spoon the orange juice mixture over the pork chops. Simmer, covered, for 45 minutes or until the chops are cooked through, stirring occasionally. Remove the chops to a platter and cover to keep warm. Bring the pan juices to a boil, stirring frequently. Spoon the sauce over the chops.

Serves 4

Nutrients Per Serving: Cal 195; Prot 20 g; Carbo 17 g; T Fat 5 g; (Saturated Fat 2 g); 24% Cal from Fat; Chol 51 mg; Fiber <1 g; Sod 50 mg; Calcium 33 mg

After the fasting of Lent, Maryland Stuffed Ham was a welcome sight on colonial tables at Easter. Today it is often served at church suppers and large gatherings.

Maryland Stuffed Ham

4 to 5 pounds kale, trimmed,
   finely chopped
1 head cabbage, finely chopped
6 to 8 onions, finely chopped
1 tablespoon red pepper

1 tablespoon celery seeds
1 tablespoon mustard seeds
2 teaspoons black pepper
1 1/2 tablespoons salt
1 (15-pound) corned ham or fresh ham

Mix the first 8 ingredients in a bowl. Make 2-inch vertical slits in the skin side of the ham. Make alternate slits across the ham. Pack the kale mixture firmly into the slits. Place the remaining kale mixture on top of the ham. Wrap the ham in cheesecloth. Place the ham in a large stockpot and add enough water to cover. Boil for 4 to 5 hours or until a meat thermometer registers an internal temperature of 160 degrees. Remove the ham from the stockpot. Chill in the refrigerator. Serve cold.

Serves 15

Nutrients Per Serving: Cal 661; Prot 88 g; Carbo 24 g; T Fat 23 g; (Saturated Fat 8 g); 32% Cal from Fat; Chol 253 mg; Fiber 6 g; Sod 947 mg; Calcium 274 mg
Nutritional profile reflects the substitution of a fresh boneless pork rump roast ham for the corned ham.

Veal with Lemon Marsala Sauce

2 (6-ounce) veal cutlets
Pepper to taste
2 tablespoons flour
1 egg, beaten
1/3 cup bread crumbs

Vegetable oil for frying
1 1/2 tablespoons margarine
3/4 cup marsala
1 teaspoon beef bouillon granules
1 large lemon, thinly sliced

Sprinkle both sides of the veal with pepper and coat with the flour. Dip into the egg and coat with the bread crumbs. Chill for 15 to 30 minutes. Heat just enough oil in a skillet to brown the veal. Fry the veal in the hot oil just until brown on both sides. Remove to a platter using a slotted spoon.

Discard most of the pan drippings. Heat the margarine with the remaining pan drippings until melted. Stir in the wine. Bring to a boil, scraping the bottom of the skillet with a wooden spoon or spatula to remove any browned bits. Add the bouillon and stir until dissolved. Return the veal to the skillet and cover with the lemon slices. Simmer, covered, for 10 to 15 minutes or until the veal is cooked through.

Serves 2

Nutrients Per Serving: Cal 737; Prot 47 g; Carbo 33 g; T Fat 35 g; (Saturated Fat 12 g); 43% Cal from Fat; Chol 263 mg; Fiber 1 g; Sod 836 mg; Calcium 115 mg
Nutritional profile does not include vegetable oil for frying.

Veal Scallopini Stew

1 1/2 pounds boneless veal
    cubes
3 green bell peppers,
    cut into quarters
2 onions, thinly sliced
8 ounces mushrooms, sliced

2 garlic cloves, or 1 teaspoon
    crushed garlic
1/2 teaspoon salt
1/2 teaspoon basil
1/2 teaspoon oregano
1 (28-ounce) can tomatoes

Combine the veal, bell peppers, onions, mushrooms, garlic, salt, basil and oregano in a slow cooker and mix well. Pour the undrained tomatoes over the top. Cook, covered, on Low for 7 hours or on High for 4 hours.

Serves 6

Nutrients Per Serving: Cal 196; Prot 24 g; Carbo 14 g; T Fat 5 g; (Saturated Fat 2 g); 22% Cal from Fat; Chol 87 mg; Fiber 4 g; Sod 464 mg; Calcium 76 mg

Eastern Shore Muskrat

Muskrat are described as "marsh rabbits" by local residents. Muskrat meat is strong, dark and delicious if properly prepared. It is considered a delicacy in many area restaurants and is served at church dinners on the Eastern Shore. Muskrat season is limited to January and February. Muskrat live in marshy areas and eat only vegetation.

2 muskrat, dressed
Salt to taste
Pepper to taste
Salt pork or bacon
2 tablespoons sage
2 tablespoons poultry seasoning
1 teaspoon crushed red pepper
Flour

Cut the muskrat into sections. Discard the fat and musk. Soak the muskrat in a large stockpot filled with salt water for 8 to 10 hours; drain. Add enough fresh water to cover the muskrat. Add the salt, pepper and salt pork. Bring to a rolling boil; drain the liquid only.

Add enough fresh water to the stockpot to cover the muskrat. Bring to a boil; reduce the heat. Cook until the muskrat are tender. Remove the muskrat to a baking pan, reserving the liquid. Sprinkle the muskrat with the sage, poultry seasoning and red pepper.

Bring the reserved liquid to a boil. Mix flour and water in a bowl until of a pasty consistency. Stir the flour mixture into the boiling liquid. Pour the boiling liquid over the muskrat. Bake, covered with foil, at 350 to 375 degrees for 1 hour. Serve with greens, hominy and corn bread.

Serves 4

Nutritional profile is not available for this recipe.

Venison Stroganoff

1 pound venison or beef tenderloin steak
Salt and pepper to taste
1/4 cup flour
2 to 3 tablespoons vegetable oil
1 tablespoon butter
6 ounces fresh mushrooms
1/2 cup chopped onion
1 (10-ounce) can beef broth
1 cup sour cream
10 ounces egg noodles, cooked, drained

Cut the venison into 1/4-inch strips. Sprinkle with salt and pepper. Coat the strips with the flour. Heat the oil and butter in a skillet. Brown the venison in the hot oil mixture.

Push the venison to the side of the skillet. Add the mushrooms and onion to the skillet. Cook until tender, stirring frequently. Stir in the broth. Bring just to a boil. Stir in the sour cream.

Cook until heated through, stirring constantly. Spoon the stroganoff over the hot cooked egg noodles on a serving platter.

Serves 5

Nutrients Per Serving: Cal 596; Prot 33 g; Carbo 50 g; T Fat 30 g; (Saturated Fat 11 g); 45% Cal from Fat; Chol 154 mg; Fiber 2 g; Sod 534 mg; Calcium 80 mg

In the fall of the year, deer hunting is quite popular in Western Maryland and on the Eastern Shore. Home and restaurant menus frequently offer venison. Is there a hunter in your family? Try this recipe.

Inistore's Sesame Chicken

1 (3-pound) chicken, quartered
1/4 cup soy sauce
2 tablespoons unsalted butter
1 1/2 teaspoons paprika
1 1/2 teaspoons curry powder
1/2 teaspoon cinnamon
1/2 teaspoon ginger
1 garlic clove, crushed
1/4 teaspoon Tabasco sauce
Sesame seeds to taste

Arrange the chicken in a single layer in a shallow glass or plastic dish. Combine the next 8 ingredients in a bowl and mix well. Spread the soy sauce mixture over both sides of the chicken. Sprinkle both sides generously with sesame seeds. Marinate, covered with plastic wrap, in the refrigerator for 1 hour. Arrange the chicken on a roasting rack in a baking pan. Roast at 250 degrees for 2 hours or until the chicken is cooked through.

Serves 4

Nutrients Per Serving: Cal 302; Prot 37 g; Carbo 2 g; T Fat 15 g; (Saturated Fat 6 g); 47% Cal from Fat; Chol 123 mg; Fiber <1 g; Sod 1426 mg; Calcium 23 mg

Broccoli and Chicken Casserole

3 (10-ounce) packages frozen broccoli spears
4 (8-ounce) boneless skinless chicken breasts, cooked, shredded
1 cup mayonnaise
1 (10-ounce) can cream of mushroom soup
1 (10-ounce) can cream of chicken soup
1/2 cup (2 ounces) shredded sharp Cheddar cheese
1 teaspoon lemon juice
1/2 teaspoon curry powder
1 cup bread crumbs
2 tablespoons butter, melted

Cook the broccoli using package directions; drain. Let stand until cool. Arrange the broccoli spears over the bottom of a 9x13-inch baking dish. Top with the chicken. Combine the next 6 ingredients in a bowl and mix well. Spoon the soup mixture over the prepared layers. Toss the bread crumbs with the butter in a bowl and sprinkle over the top. Bake at 350 degrees for 45 minutes. Broil for 1 minute or until brown.

Serves 8

Nutrients Per Serving: Cal 484; Prot 22 g; Carbo 21 g; T Fat 35 g; (Saturated Fat 9 g); 65% Cal from Fat; Chol 75 mg; Fiber 4 g; Sod 952 mg; Calcium 153 mg

Chicken Pesto Pasta

8 ounces gemelli
12 ounces boneless skinless chicken breasts, cut into 1-inch pieces
Salt and pepper to taste
1 tablespoon olive oil
1 tablespoon finely chopped garlic
3/4 cup Homemade Pesto (below) or commercially prepared pesto

Cook the pasta using package directions; drain. Cover to keep warm. Sprinkle the chicken with salt and pepper. Heat the olive oil in a skillet over medium heat. Add the chicken and garlic to the hot olive oil. Cook for 5 minutes or until the chicken is cooked through, stirring occasionally. Toss the hot pasta, pesto and chicken in a bowl. Serve immediately. Double the recipe for a large crowd.

Makes 5 (1-cup) servings

Nutrients Per Serving: Cal 560; Prot 34 g; Carbo 56 g; T Fat 23 g; (Saturated Fat 4 g); 36% Cal from Fat; Chol 41 mg; Fiber 19 g; Sod 222 mg; Calcium 1148 mg

Homemade Pesto

2 ounces mild Parmesan cheese
6 cups lightly packed fresh basil leaves
2/3 to 3/4 cup olive oil
1/2 cup fresh parsley leaves
1/2 cup pine nuts or other mild nuts
2 medium or 4 small garlic cloves, chopped
1/2 teaspoon salt

Process the cheese in a food processor until grated. Add the basil, olive oil, parsley, pine nuts, garlic and salt. Process to the desired consistency. Chill, covered, in a bowl for 24 hours or longer to allow the flavors to marry. You may freeze in individual portions or in ice cube trays. Remove the frozen cubes and store in a sealable plastic freezer bag.

Makes 8 (1/4-cup) servings

Nutrients Per Serving: Cal 492; Prot 24 g; Carbo 37 g; T Fat 29 g; (Saturated Fat 5 g); 52% Cal from Fat; Chol 6 mg; Fiber 29 g; Sod 311 mg; Calcium 1884 mg

Mexican Chicken

1 (6-ounce) package Mexican
   rice
12 ounces boneless skinless
   chicken breasts, cubed

1/2 to 1 teaspoon garlic powder
1/2 to 1 teaspoon cumin
1 (16-ounce) can pinto beans in
   chili sauce

Prepare the rice using package directions. Brown the chicken with the garlic powder and cumin in a nonstick skillet. Stir in the rice and beans. Cook until heated through, stirring frequently. Serve with a mixed green or fruit salad.

Serves 4

Nutrients Per Serving: Cal 341; Prot 26 g; Carbo 49 g; T Fat 3 g; (Saturated Fat 1 g); 9% Cal from Fat; Chol 47 mg; Fiber 7 g; Sod 989 mg; Calcium 35 mg

Chicken Stir-Fry with Cabbage

2 tablespoons olive oil
1 tablespoon soy sauce
1 tablespoon honey
1/4 teaspoon ginger
2 cups chopped boneless
   skinless chicken breasts
4 to 5 cups shredded cabbage
1 onion, cut into thin wedges

2 cups broccoli florets
1 (8-ounce) can sliced water
   chestnuts, drained
1 (16-ounce) can mixed Chinese
   vegetables, drained
1 chicken bouillon cube
1/2 cup hot water
2 tablespoons cornstarch

Mix the first 4 ingredients in a shallow glass dish. Stir in the chicken. Marinate at room temperature for 15 to 20 minutes, stirring occasionally. Stir-fry the undrained chicken in a wok for 10 minutes or just until cooked through. Remove the chicken with a slotted spoon to a platter, reserving the pan drippings. Stir-fry the cabbage and onion in the reserved pan drippings for 10 minutes. Stir in the broccoli and water chestnuts.

Stir-fry for 6 minutes. Stir in the Chinese vegetables. Stir-fry until heated through. Add the chicken and mix well. Dissolve the bouillon cube in the hot water and mix well. Stir the cornstarch into the bouillon. Add the cornstarch mixture to the chicken mixture and mix well. Stir-fry just until heated through.

Serves 4

Nutrients Per Serving: Cal 294; Prot 26 g; Carbo 27 g; T Fat 10 g; (Saturated Fat 2 g); 30% Cal from Fat; Chol 59 mg; Fiber 8 g; Sod 761 mg; Calcium 93 mg

Oriental-Style Chicken Stew

3 pounds chicken pieces
1 cup water
$^1/_3$ cup vinegar
2 tablespoons soy sauce
1 tablespoon crushed garlic
2 bay leaves, crushed
$^1/_2$ teaspoon ground pepper
1 tablespoon vegetable oil

Arrange the chicken in a single layer in a shallow glass or plastic dish. Combine the water, vinegar, soy sauce, garlic, bay leaves and pepper in a bowl and mix well. Pour the soy sauce mixture over the chicken, turning to coat. Marinate, covered with plastic wrap, in the refrigerator for 1 hour, turning occasionally.

Place the undrained chicken mixture in a saucepan. Bring to a boil; reduce the heat. Simmer for 20 minutes or until the chicken is cooked through. Add additional water if the chicken is not tender after 20 minutes and continue to simmer until cooked through. Remove the chicken with a slotted spoon to a plate, reserving the pan juices. Cover to keep warm.

Heat the oil in a skillet. Brown the chicken on both sides in the hot oil. Transfer the chicken to a platter. Drizzle with the reserved pan juices.

Serves 8

Nutrients Per Serving: Cal 145; Prot 20 g; Carbo 2 g; T Fat 6 g; (Saturated Fat 1 g); 37% Cal from Fat; Chol 59 mg; Fiber <1 g; Sod 384 mg; Calcium 11 mg

This is a traditional and favorite Filipino recipe. For variety, substitute pork for the chicken and enjoy!

Murgh Hyderabadi (Chicken Hyderabad Style)

1 (3-inch) cinnamon stick
3 garlic cloves, crushed
1 ounce fresh gingerroot, chopped
2 fresh green chiles, thinly sliced
6 peppercorns
4 whole cloves
3 cardamom pods, crushed
1 cup plain yogurt
1 1/2 teaspoons turmeric
1 onion, chopped
1/4 cup (1/2 stick) butter
3 pounds chicken pieces (8 pieces)
3 tomatoes, chopped
Salt to taste
Chopped fresh cilantro to taste

Combine the cinnamon stick, garlic, gingerroot, green chiles, peppercorns, whole cloves and cardamom in a bowl and mix well. Mix the yogurt and turmeric in a small bowl.

Sauté the onion in the butter in a skillet until golden brown. Add the garlic mixture, or full masala. Sauté for 2 minutes. Add the chicken.

Sauté for 2 minutes longer. Stir in the tomatoes and salt. Add the yogurt mixture and mix well. Simmer, covered, for 20 minutes or until the chicken is cooked through, stirring occasionally. Sprinkle with cilantro before serving.

Makes 4 (2-piece) servings

Nutrients Per Serving: Cal 475; Prot 48 g; Carbo 13 g; T Fat 25 g; (Saturated Fat 12 g); 48% Cal from Fat; Chol 180 mg; Fiber 2 g; Sod 281 mg; Calcium 117 mg

Chicken and Dumplings

5 cups chicken broth
$1/2$ cup sliced celery
$1/2$ cup sliced carrots
1 bay leaf
1 teaspoon parsley flakes
2 cups baking mix
$1/4$ teaspoon thyme
$1/8$ teaspoon nutmeg
$2/3$ cup milk
$1/2$ teaspoon parsley flakes
3 cups chopped cooked chicken or turkey

Combine the broth, celery, carrots, bay leaf and 1 teaspoon parsley flakes in a 5-quart Dutch oven. Bring to a boil.

Combine the baking mix, thyme and nutmeg in a bowl and mix well. Add the milk and $1/2$ teaspoon parsley flakes and stir until a dough forms. Drop the dough by tablespoonfuls into the boiling broth mixture. Cook for 10 minutes. Cover and cook for 10 minutes longer.

Remove the dumplings to a serving bowl using a slotted spoon. Bring the broth to a boil. Stir in the chicken. Cook just until heated through, stirring occasionally. Discard the bay leaf. Pour the chicken mixture over the dumplings.

Makes 4 (1-cup) servings

Nutrients Per Serving: Cal 538; Prot 44 g; Carbo 65 g; T Fat 11 g; (Saturated Fat 3 g); 19% Cal from Fat; Chol 84 mg; Fiber 5 g; Sod 1727 mg; Calcium 183 mg

Baked Chicken with Rice and Vegetables

1 (14-ounce) can chicken broth
1 (10-ounce) can cream of mushroom soup
1/3 cup lite sour cream
1 (16-ounce) package frozen California-blend vegetables
1 (10-ounce) can white meat chicken, drained
1 1/2 cups instant brown rice
1 teaspoon onion flakes
10 twists freshly ground pepper

Combine the broth, soup and sour cream in a large bowl and mix well. Stir in the vegetables, chicken, rice, onion flakes and pepper. Spoon into a 9x13-inch baking dish.

Bake, covered, at 375 degrees for 45 minutes. Remove the cover. Bake for 10 minutes longer.

You may substitute reduced-fat cream of mushroom soup for the mushroom soup and reduced-sodium chicken broth for the chicken broth.

Serves 4

Nutrients Per Serving: Cal 372; Prot 26 g; Carbo 40 g; T Fat 11 g; (Saturated Fat 4 g); 27% Cal from Fat; Chol 40 mg; Fiber 4 g; Sod 1495 mg; Calcium 80 mg

Chicken Lasagna

1/2 cup finely chopped onion
1/4 cup finely chopped green bell pepper
2 tablespoons butter
1 (10-ounce) can cream of mushroom or cream of chicken soup
2/3 cup milk
8 ounces lasagna noodles, cooked, drained
2 cups small curd cottage cheese
8 ounces cream cheese, cut into 1/2-inch cubes
2 1/2 cups chopped cooked chicken
3 cups (12 ounces) shredded Cheddar cheese
1/4 cup grated Parmesan cheese

Sauté the onion and bell pepper in the butter in a skillet until tender. Stir in the soup and milk. Spread the bottom of a 9x13-inch baking pan with just enough of the soup mixture to cover.

Layer the noodles, cottage cheese, cream cheese, chicken, Cheddar cheese and soup mixture 1/3 at a time in the prepared baking pan. Sprinkle with the Parmesan cheese. Bake at 350 degrees for 50 to 60 minutes or until bubbly. You may prepare 1 day in advance and store, covered, in the refrigerator. Bake just before serving.

Serves 12

Nutrients Per Serving: Cal 397; Prot 25 g; Carbo 19 g; T Fat 25 g; (Saturated Fat 14 g); 56% Cal from Fat; Chol 87 mg; Fiber 1 g; Sod 639 mg; Calcium 297 mg

Lasagna can be assembled one day in advance, chilled, and baked the following day. Even better, double the recipe and store one lasagna in the freezer for future use. Free up some time from cooking every night.

Chicken Potpie

2 refrigerator pie pastries
1 (16-ounce) package frozen mixed vegetables
12 ounces chopped cooked chicken
1 (10-ounce) can cream of chicken or cream of mushroom soup
1 potato, boiled, chopped
1 onion, sliced

Fit 1 of the pie pastries into a baking dish. Combine the mixed vegetables, chicken, soup, potato and onion in a bowl and mix gently. Spoon the chicken mixture into the prepared baking dish.

Top the chicken mixture with the remaining pie pastry, crimping the edges and cutting vents. Bake, covered with foil, at 350 degrees for 30 minutes; remove the foil. Bake for 15 minutes longer or until light brown.

Serves 8

Nutrients Per Serving: Cal 400; Prot 16 g; Carbo 41 g; T Fat 19 g; (Saturated Fat 7 g); 43% Cal from Fat; Chol 45 mg; Fiber 3 g; Sod 558 mg; Calcium 35 mg

Fresh vegetables do not necessarily contain more nutrients than frozen vegetables. Frozen vegetables typically are processed at their peak and therefore may have even more nutrients. The nutritional quality of fresh vegetables depends on the care given the vegetables after harvest. . . . from the field to your table. If produce is stored improperly or too long, nutrients may be lost.

Spicy Skillet Chicken Supper

1 medium zucchini
1 tablespoon olive oil
1 cup long grain converted rice
2 garlic cloves, minced
1 (14-ounce) can stewed tomatoes
1 (14-ounce) can chicken broth
1 tablespoon chili powder
1 teaspoon cumin
1/2 teaspoon salt
1 1/2 cups chopped cooked chicken or turkey
1/2 cup (1/2-inch) slices green onions with tops
1 cup (4 ounces) shredded low-fat Cheddar cheese

Cut the zucchini horizontally into halves and cut each half into slices. Heat the olive oil in a large skillet over medium-high heat. Stir in the rice and garlic. Cook for 2 minutes or until the rice is light brown, stirring constantly. Add the undrained tomatoes, broth, chili powder, cumin and salt and mix well. Bring to a boil; reduce the heat.

Simmer, covered, for 15 minutes, stirring occasionally. Add the zucchini, chicken and green onions and mix gently. Simmer, covered, for 10 minutes, stirring occasionally. Remove from heat. Let stand for 5 minutes or until the liquid is absorbed. Sprinkle with the cheese. Let stand, covered, for 2 minutes or until the cheese melts.

Serves 4

Nutrients Per Serving: Cal 414; Prot 30 g; Carbo 50 g; T Fat 10 g; (Saturated Fat 3 g); 23% Cal from Fat; Chol 46 mg; Fiber 3 g; Sod 1367 mg; Calcium 204 mg

No more boring leftovers! This is a fantastic recipe for using leftover poultry and garden-fresh zucchini. If you don't like zucchini, try substituting another vegetable.

Wild Rice-Stuffed Turkey Breast

Serve Spiced Cranberry Sauce with Zinfandel as an accompaniment. Combine 1³/4 cups red zinfandel, 1 cup sugar, 1 cup packed brown sugar, 6 whole cloves, 6 whole allspice, 2 cinnamon sticks and 1 (1x3-inch) strip orange zest in a saucepan. Bring to a boil over medium-high heat. Boil until the sugar dissolves, stirring constantly. Simmer for 10 minutes. Strain the syrup into a saucepan, discarding the solids. Stir in 12 ounces fresh cranberries. Cook over medium heat for 6 minutes or until the cranberries burst. Let stand until cool. Chill, covered, until serving time.

1 (3-ounce) package dried
   cranberries
2 cups port
2 cups chicken broth
1/2 cup long grain rice
1/2 cup wild rice
1 small onion, chopped
1/2 cup chopped celery
1 teaspoon pepper
2 cups soft whole wheat bread
   crumbs
1 (6-pound) turkey breast
2 teaspoons chopped fresh
   rosemary
2 garlic cloves, minced
1 tablespoon kosher salt
1 tablespoon freshly ground
   pepper
2 tablespoons butter or
   margarine
3 tablespoons flour
11/2 cups chicken broth

Combine the cranberries and wine in a glass or plastic bowl and mix well. Let stand for 1 hour. Drain, reserving the wine. Bring 2 cups broth, long grain rice, wild rice, onion, celery and 1 teaspoon pepper to a boil in a medium saucepan, stirring occasionally; reduce the heat. Simmer, covered, for 30 minutes or until the liquid is absorbed and the rice is tender. Let stand until cool. Stir in the cranberries and bread crumbs.

Remove the bone from the turkey breast by inserting a knife between the breast meat and bone, leaving the skin and meat intact. Place the turkey breast between 2 sheets of heavy-duty plastic wrap. Pound 1 inch thick with a meat mallet or a rolling pin. Rub the skinless side of the turkey with the rosemary and garlic. Spread with the rice mixture. Roll as for a jelly roll beginning at the long side. Secure with kitchen twine at 2-inch intervals. Sprinkle with the salt and 1 tablespoon pepper.

Arrange the turkey roll on a rack sprayed with nonstick cooking spray. Place the rack in a roasting pan. Bake at 375 degrees for 2 hours or until a meat thermometer registers 180 degrees. Remove the turkey roll to a platter, reserving the pan drippings. Let stand for 10 minutes.

Heat the butter in a heavy saucepan over low heat. Stir in the reserved pan drippings. Whisk in the flour until smooth. Cook for 1 minute, whisking constantly. Add the reserved wine and 11/2 cups broth gradually, whisking constantly. Cook over medium heat for 5 minutes or until of a sauce consistency, whisking frequently. Serve the wine sauce with the turkey.

Serves 10

Nutrients Per Serving: Cal 556; Prot 76 g; Carbo 34 g; T Fat 5 g; (Saturated Fat 2 g); 9% Cal from Fat; Chol 203 mg; Fiber 2 g; Sod 1046 mg; Calcium 54 mg

Mexican Turkey Loaf

1 pound ground turkey
1/2 cup salsa
1/2 cup (2 ounces) shredded Cheddar cheese
1/4 cup chopped hot chiles or jalapeño chiles
1/2 cup broken tortilla chips
1/2 cup (2 ounces) shredded mozzarella cheese

Combine the ground turkey, salsa, Cheddar cheese and hot chiles in a bowl and mix well. Shape the turkey mixture into a loaf in a greased loaf pan. Sprinkle with the chips and mozzarella cheese.

Bake at 350 degrees for 35 to 45 minutes or until cooked through and brown. Reduce the fat grams and sodium levels by using low-sodium low-fat Cheddar cheese and low-sodium low-fat mozzarella cheese.

Serves 4

Nutrients Per Serving: Cal 348; Prot 30 g; Carbo 10 g; T Fat 21 g; (Saturated Fat 8 g); 55% Cal from Fat; Chol 108 mg; Fiber 1 g; Sod 420 mg; Calcium 221 mg

Savory Black Beans

2 teaspoons olive oil
1 cup chopped onion
2 garlic cloves, minced
2 (14-ounce) cans diced tomatoes, drained
1 (4-ounce) can diced mild green chiles, drained
2 (15-ounce) cans black beans, drained, rinsed
2 cups frozen corn
1/4 cup chopped fresh cilantro
1 teaspoon cumin
1/2 teaspoon red pepper
1/4 teaspoon chili powder
1/8 teaspoon salt
3 cups hot cooked brown rice

Heat the olive oil in a nonstick skillet over medium-high heat. Sauté the onion and garlic in the hot olive oil until the onion is tender. Stir in the tomatoes and green chiles; reduce the heat.

Cook for 6 to 8 minutes or until slightly thickened, stirring occasionally. Add the beans, corn, cilantro, cumin, red pepper, chili powder and salt and mix well. Cook, covered, for 5 minutes or until heated through, stirring occasionally. Spoon over the rice. Omit the rice and serve with baked tortilla chips or wrap the black bean mixture in a tortilla for a black bean burrito for variety.

Makes 6 (1-cup) servings

Nutrients Per Serving: Cal 324; Prot 12 g; Carbo 64 g; T Fat 3 g; (Saturated Fat <1 g); 8% Cal from Fat; Chol 0 mg; Fiber 12 g; Sod 893 mg; Calcium 87 mg

Cheesy Egg Casserole

1/2 cup flour
1 teaspoon baking powder
1/8 teaspoon salt
6 eggs
1 cup milk
1 cup cottage cheese
16 ounces Monterey Jack cheese, cubed
3 ounces cream cheese, cubed
2 tablespoons butter

Mix the flour, baking powder and salt. Beat the eggs in a mixing bowl until blended. Add the flour mixture and milk and beat until smooth. Beat in the cottage cheese. Stir in the Monterey Jack cheese and cream cheese.

Pour the egg mixture into a greased and floured 2-quart baking dish. Dot with the butter. Bake at 350 degrees for 45 minutes.

Serves 6

Nutrients Per Serving: Cal 542; Prot 33 g; Carbo 13 g; T Fat 40 g; (Saturated Fat 23 g); 66% Cal from Fat; Chol 317 mg; Fiber <1 g; Sod 851 mg; Calcium 718 mg

Make this recipe heart-healthy by the use of the following ingredients: 12 egg whites or 1 1/2 cups egg substitute, fat-free cottage cheese, fat-free cream cheese, and low-fat Monterey Jack cheese. Omit the salt and butter and spray the top of the casserole with a low-fat or nonfat nonstick baking spray.

Overnight French Toast

1 loaf French or Italian bread
3 cups milk
3 eggs
1 tablespoon vanilla extract
4 teaspoons sugar
3/4 teaspoon salt
2 tablespoons butter
4 teaspoons cinnamon

Cut the loaf into 3/4-inch slices. Arrange the bread slices cut side down in a greased 9x13-inch baking pan. Beat the milk, eggs, vanilla, sugar and salt in a mixing bowl until blended. Pour the egg mixture over the bread. Cover and refrigerate overnight.

Remove the cover and dot with the butter. Sprinkle with the cinnamon. Bake at 350 degrees for 45 minutes. Cut into squares and serve immediately with warm maple syrup.

Serves 8

Nutrients Per Serving: Cal 281; Prot 10 g; Carbo 37 g; T Fat 10 g; (Saturated Fat 5 g); 31% Cal from Fat; Chol 100 mg; Fiber 2 g; Sod 661 mg; Calcium 172 mg

Creamy Garden Spaghetti

8 ounces broccoli florets
1½ cups sliced zucchini
1½ cups sliced fresh
    mushrooms
1 large carrot, sliced
1 tablespoon olive oil
8 ounces spaghetti
¼ cup chopped onion
3 garlic cloves, minced
2 tablespoons margarine

2 tablespoons flour
2 teaspoons chicken bouillon
    granules
1 teaspoon thyme
2 cups fat-free or low-fat milk
½ cup (2 ounces) shredded
    Swiss cheese
½ cup (2 ounces) shredded
    mozzarella cheese

Sauté the broccoli, zucchini, mushrooms and carrot in the olive oil in a skillet until tender-crisp. Remove from the heat. Cook the spaghetti using package directions; drain. Cover to keep warm.

Sauté the onion and garlic in the margarine in a large saucepan until the onion is tender. Stir in the flour, bouillon and thyme. Cook until bubbly, stirring constantly. Add the fat-free milk gradually, stirring constantly. Bring to a boil. Cook for 2 minutes or until thickened, stirring constantly. Reduce the heat to low.

Add the Swiss cheese and mozzarella cheese to the sauce and mix well. Cook until the cheese melts, stirring constantly. Fold in the sautéed vegetables. Cook just until heated through, stirring occasionally. Add the pasta and toss until mixed.

Serves 4

Nutrients Per Serving: Cal 486; Prot 22 g; Carbo 61 g; T Fat 17 g; (Saturated Fat 6 g); 32% Cal from Fat; Chol 26 mg; Fiber 5 g; Sod 822 mg; Calcium 416 mg

Mild olive oil *is a blend of virgin and refined oils, has a golden color, milder taste, and is good for pastas, sauces, and stir-fry dishes.* Light olive oil, *with the smallest percentage of virgin olive oil, has a very mild color and flavor. Use it as a substitute for other vegetable oils to fry, sauté, and even bake.*

Spaghetti with Spinach Sauce

4 to 6 quarts water
2 tablespoons salt
16 ounces spaghetti
1 cup firmly packed fresh spinach leaves
1/4 cup firmly packed fresh parsley leaves
1/4 cup (1/2 stick) butter or margarine, melted
1/4 cup freshly grated Romano cheese
1/4 cup freshly grated Parmesan cheese
1/4 cup olive oil
1/4 cup pine nuts
2 tablespoons chopped walnuts
1 garlic clove
3/4 teaspoon salt
1/2 teaspoon basil

Bring the water to boil in a large saucepan. Stir in 2 tablespoons salt. Add the pasta gradually, stirring constantly. Cook until tender, stirring occasionally. Drain in a colander, reserving 2 tablespoons of the water. Cover the pasta to keep warm.

Rinse the spinach and parsley. Shake to remove only the excess moisture, allowing some moisture to cling to the leaves. Combine the spinach, parsley, butter, Romano cheese, Parmesan cheese, olive oil, pine nuts, walnuts, garlic, 3/4 teaspoon salt and basil in a blender.

Process at high speed to the consistency of a thick purée with specks of spinach and parsley still visible. Add the desired amount of the reserved pasta water for a thinner consistency. Add the spinach sauce to the pasta in a bowl and toss until coated.

Serves 6

Nutrients Per Serving: Cal 512; Prot 15 g; Carbo 59 g; T Fat 25 g; (Saturated Fat 8 g); 43% Cal from Fat; Chol 28 mg; Fiber 3 g; Sod 2823 mg; Calcium 128 mg

Zucchini Lasagna

3 or 4 medium zucchini
8 ounces ground turkey
1/2 cup chopped onion
1 (15-ounce) can tomato sauce
1/2 teaspoon oregano
1/4 teaspoon basil
1/8 teaspoon salt
1/8 teaspoon pepper
1 cup low-fat small curd cottage cheese
1 egg, lightly beaten
2 tablespoons flour
1 cup (4 ounces) shredded mozzarella cheese

Cut the zucchini horizontally into 1/4-inch sections resembling lasagna noodles. Brown the ground turkey with the onion in a nonstick skillet, stirring until the ground turkey is crumbly; drain. Stir in the tomato sauce, oregano, basil, salt and pepper. Bring to a boil; reduce the heat. Simmer for 10 to 15 minutes or until of a sauce consistency, stirring occasionally. Combine the cottage cheese and egg in a bowl and mix well.

Layer 1/2 of the sliced zucchini in a 9×12-inch baking dish. Sprinkle with 1 tablespoon of the flour. Spread with 1/2 of the cottage cheese mixture and 1/2 of the sauce. Layer the remaining zucchini and remaining flour over the prepared layers. Spread with the remaining cottage cheese mixture and 1/2 of the remaining sauce. Sprinkle with the mozzarella cheese and spread with the remaining sauce. Bake at 375 degrees for 40 to 50 minutes or until bubbly. Let stand for 10 minutes before serving.

Serves 4

Nutrients Per Serving: Cal 318; Prot 29 g; Carbo 21 g; T Fat 14 g; (Saturated Fat 6 g); 39% Cal from Fat; Chol 124 mg; Fiber 4 g; Sod 1076 mg; Calcium 250 mg

Do not let the word "turkey" fool you into thinking that ground turkey is always lower in fat than ground beef. Look for the words "ground turkey breast" to ensure you are buying the leanest source of ground turkey. Also check the ingredient list for added turkey skin, which will also add extra fat.

Tomato Sauce with Prosciutto and Mushrooms

1 (15-ounce) can tomato sauce
4 ounces prosciutto, chopped
1 medium onion, chopped
Basil to taste
Oregano to taste
Pepper to taste
1 pound fresh mushrooms, trimmed, sliced

Combine the tomato sauce, prosciutto, onion, basil, oregano and pepper in a saucepan and mix well. Simmer over low heat for 15 minutes, stirring occasionally. Stir in the mushrooms.

Cook until heated through, stirring frequently. Spoon over your favorite hot cooked pasta in a pasta bowl.

Serves 4

Nutrients Per Serving: Cal 130; Prot 13 g; Carbo 14 g; T Fat 4 g; (Saturated Fat 1 g); 24% Cal from Fat; Chol 25 mg; Fiber 3 g; Sod 1189 mg; Calcium 20 mg
Nutritional profile does not include pasta.

The prosciutto in this recipe perks up the flavor, making it special. Since the ingredients are easy to pack, take them along for a quick dinner after a day at the beach. Ocean City and nearby Assateague Island, both in Worcester County, offer great opportunities to walk, bike, and swim. Healthy eating and great exercise! Try to see the sunrise at least once. A spectacular sight as the sun rises over the ocean!

Roquefort and Prosciutto Pasta

8 ounces thinly sliced prosciutto, chopped
1/3 pound Roquefort cheese or bleu cheese, crumbled
2 cups large walnut pieces, chopped
1 cup chopped fresh Italian parsley
1/4 cup finely chopped fresh rosemary
2 garlic cloves, minced
11/2 teaspoons freshly ground pepper
1/2 cup (or less) olive oil
16 ounces linguini or angel hair pasta
Freshly grated Parmesan cheese to taste

Combine the prosciutto, Roquefort cheese, walnuts, parsley, rosemary, garlic and pepper in a bowl and mix well. Stir in the olive oil. Let stand at room temperature for 4 hours, stirring occasionally.

Cook the pasta using package directions; drain. Toss the pasta with the sauce in a bowl immediately. Serve with Parmesan cheese. You may substitute chopped baked ham for the prosciutto.

Serves 8

Nutrients Per Serving: Cal 570; Prot 21 g; Carbo 36 g; T Fat 40 g; (Saturated Fat 8 g); 61% Cal from Fat; Chol 42 mg; Fiber 4 g; Sod 992 mg; Calcium 164 mg

Vegetarian Stuffed Sweet Peppers

4 green bell peppers
1 (14-ounce) package instant brown rice
1 (15-ounce) can black beans, rinsed, drained
1 (15-ounce) can garbanzo beans, drained
1 (14-ounce) can diced tomatoes
Bread crumbs (optional)
Grated Parmesan cheese (optional)

Cut the top off each bell pepper, reserving the tops. Remove the seeds and membranes from the bell peppers. Chop the edible portion of the reserved tops and set aside.

Parboil the bell peppers in a saucepan in boiling water for 5 minutes or just until tender; drain. Prepare the rice using package directions. Add the reserved chopped bell pepper, beans, and undrained tomatoes to the rice and mix well.

Arrange the bell peppers cut side up in a baking dish. Fill each bell pepper with some of the rice mixture. Sprinkle with bread crumbs and cheese. Spoon the remaining rice mixture into the baking dish. Bake at 350 degrees for 30 minutes. Serve immediately.

Serves 4

Nutrients Per Serving: Cal 671; Prot 21 g; Carbo 121 g; T Fat 11 g; (Saturated Fat 4 g); 14% Cal from Fat; Chol 16 mg; Fiber 17 g; Sod 866 mg; Calcium 95 mg

Traditionally, stuffed sweet peppers were only green and red. Today, these mild peppers can be yellow, orange, or even purple. Interestingly, all peppers start out green and turn other colors as they ripen.

Tofu Nut Balls

8 ounces firm tofu, crumbled
1 cup walnuts, finely chopped
1 cup whole wheat cracker crumbs
1 packet any flavor G. Washington Seasoning & Broth mix
Vegetable oil for frying

Combine the tofu, walnuts, cracker crumbs and seasoning in a bowl and mix well. Shape the tofu mixture into 4 patties or small balls. Fry in 1/2 inch oil in a skillet until light brown; drain.

The patties may be arranged in a baking dish and covered with your favorite sauce or gravy. Bake at 350 degrees for 30 minutes or until heated through. Or the patties may be placed between 2 slices of your favorite bread for a sandwich. You may freeze for future use. Reheat in the microwave.

Serves 4

Nutrients Per Serving: Cal 303; Prot 10 g; Carbo 21 g; T Fat 22 g; (Saturated Fat 3 g); 62% Cal from Fat; Chol 0 mg; Fiber 4 g; Sod 176 mg; Calcium 54 mg
Nutritional profile does not include G. Washington Seasoning and Broth.
Nutritional profile does not include oil for frying.

Tofu is made from soybeans in a process similar to the production of dairy cheese. Tofu is cholesterol-free, low in saturated fat, and high in protein. It is rather bland and tasteless and absorbs the flavors of the foods with which it is combined. Tofu is usually found in the produce section of most supermarkets.

Zucchini Cakes

Today, there is more to a vegetarian diet than sprouts and soy burgers. Supermarket shelves are full of exciting grains, pastas, spices, and other vegetarian-friendly items. This is a delicious alternative to the traditional crab cake.

2¹/2 cups shredded peeled zucchini
1 cup bread crumbs
¹/4 cup chopped onion
¹/4 cup flour
1 egg, lightly beaten
1 tablespoon Old Bay seasoning
Olive oil for frying

Drain the zucchini on paper towels and pat dry. Combine the zucchini, bread crumbs, onion, flour, egg and Old Bay seasoning in a bowl and mix well. Shape the zucchini mixture into 8 cakes.

Fry the cakes in hot olive oil in a skillet until brown on both sides; drain. Arrange the cakes on a broiler rack. Broil for 5 minutes or until heated through.

Makes 4 (2-cake) servings

Nutrients Per Serving: Cal 168; Prot 7 g; Carbo 29 g; T Fat 3 g; (Saturated Fat 1 g);
16% Cal from Fat; Chol 53 mg; Fiber 2 g; Sod 746 mg; Calcium 82 mg
Nutritional profile does not include olive oil for frying.

Seafood

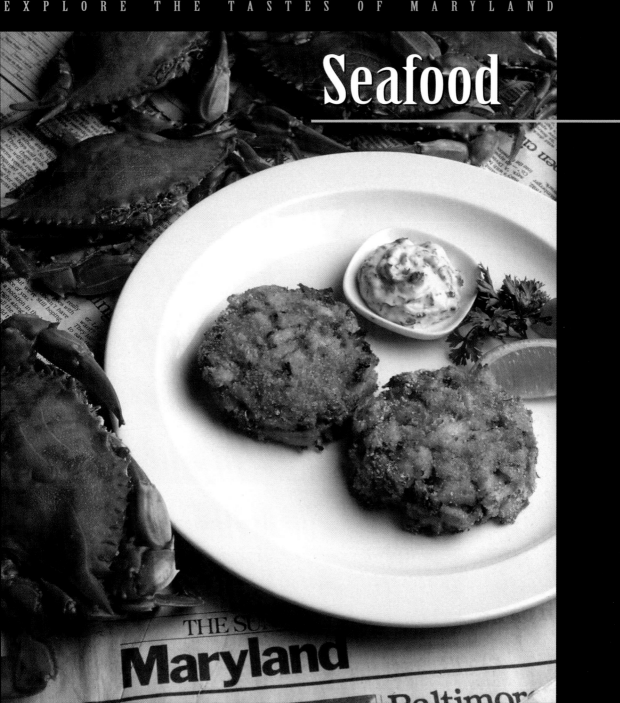

Seafood

Striped Bass in White Wine

3 tablespoons butter, softened
1 1/2 cups dry white wine
1/2 cup water
1/2 cup finely chopped onion
1 carrot, peeled, sliced
2 sprigs of parsley
1 garlic clove
12 peppercorns

1 bay leaf
1/2 teaspoon thyme
Salt to taste
1 (3- to 4-pound) striped bass,
    cleaned, scaled
3 tablespoons flour
3 tablespoons butter, softened
Juice of 1 lemon

Brush the side and bottom of a fish poacher or Dutch oven with 3 tablespoons butter. Add the wine, water, onion, carrot, parsley, garlic, peppercorns, bay leaf, thyme and salt to the prepared pan and mix well. Bring to a boil. Arrange the bass over the vegetable mixture.

Simmer, covered, for 15 to 18 minutes or until the bass flakes easily with a fork. Remove the bass carefully to a serving platter. Strain the liquid into a saucepan, discarding the solids.

Mix the flour and 3 tablespoons butter in a bowl until smooth. Bring the strained liquid to a boil. Add the butter mixture gradually, stirring constantly. Cook until thickened and of a sauce consistency, stirring constantly. Stir in the lemon juice. Serve the sauce with the fish.

Serves 8

Nutrients Per Serving: Cal 357; Prot 43 g; Carbo 5 g; T Fat 14 g; (Saturated Fat 7 g); 37% Cal from Fat; Chol 215 mg; Fiber 1 g; Sod 257 mg; Calcium 47 mg

Did you know? The alcohol from the wine used in this recipe will evaporate in the cooking process, leaving behind its wonderful light flavor. Maryland's grape growers harvest about 450 tons of grapes and our wineries produce more than 300,000 bottles of wine each year. If you occasionally appreciate a good bottle of wine, visit the annual Maryland Wine Festival, held the third weekend in September at the Carroll County Farm Museum in Westminster.

Crab-Stuffed Rockfish

3 tablespoons butter
1/2 cup finely chopped celery
1/4 cup finely chopped green
  onions
1/4 cup flour
3/4 cup clam juice
1/2 cup (or more) cream
3 tablespoons lemon juice
Salt and black pepper to taste
Cayenne pepper to taste
1 cup dry bread crumbs
1/2 to 1 cup crab meat

1 egg yolk, beaten
1 tablespoon finely chopped
  fresh parsley
1 (3- to 4-pound) rockfish,
  boned, butterflied
1/4 cup white wine
2 tablespoons butter
5 tablespoons grated Parmesan
  cheese (optional)
3 tablespoons bread crumbs
  (optional)
2 tablespoons paprika (optional)

Heat 3 tablespoons butter in a skillet. Sauté the celery and green onions in the butter until tender but not brown. Stir in the flour. Cook for 2 minutes, stirring constantly. Add the clam juice, cream and lemon juice and mix well. Bring to a boil; reduce the heat.

Simmer for several minutes, stirring occasionally. Season with salt, black pepper and cayenne pepper. Stir in 1 cup bread crumbs and the crab meat. Add the egg yolk and parsley and mix well. Let stand until cool.

Fill the cavity of the fish with the crab meat mixture. Arrange the fish in a buttered baking dish. Pour the wine over the fish. Dot with 2 tablespoons butter. Bake at 400 degrees for 25 minutes. Remove the top skin of the fish toward the end of the cooking process if desired and sprinkle with the cheese, 3 tablespoons bread crumbs and paprika. Bake until brown and the fish flakes easily with a fork.

Serves 8

Nutrients Per Serving: Cal 432; Prot 49 g; Carbo 15 g; T Fat 18 g; (Saturated Fat 9 g); 38% Cal from Fat; Chol 159 mg; Fiber 1 g; Sod 425 mg; Calcium 89 mg

Salmon with Baby Spinach, Red Pepper and Onion

4 cups baby spinach, stems removed
1 medium onion, cut into thin wedges
1 tablespoon olive oil or vegetable oil
1 tablespoon jalapeño jelly
1 small red or yellow bell pepper, cut into thin strips
1 (1-pound) salmon fillet
1/4 teaspoon salt
1/4 teaspoon pepper
2 tablespoons olive oil or vegetable oil
3 tablespoons jalapeño jelly
1 tablespoon balsamic vinegar

Place the spinach in a bowl. Sauté the onion in 1 tablespoon olive oil in a skillet over medium-high heat until tender and light brown. Stir in 1 tablespoon jalapeño jelly. Add the bell pepper and mix well. Cook for 1 minute longer, stirring frequently. Stir the onion mixture into the spinach. Cover and set aside.

Cut the fillet into 4 equal portions. Sprinkle with the salt and pepper. Heat 2 tablespoons olive oil in a skillet over medium-high heat. Add the salmon. Cook for 2 minutes per side to sear. Reduce the heat to medium.

Cook for 5 minutes longer or until the salmon flakes easily with a fork. Remove the salmon to a serving platter, reserving the pan drippings. Cover to keep warm. Stir 3 tablespoons jalapeño jelly into the reserved pan drippings. Cook until the jelly melts, stirring frequently. Drizzle over the salmon. Toss the spinach mixture with the balsamic vinegar just before serving and serve with the salmon.

Serves 4

Nutrients Per Serving: Cal 339; Prot 23 g; Carbo 19 g; T Fat 19 g; (Saturated Fat 3 g); 50% Cal from Fat; Chol 68 mg; Fiber 2 g; Sod 228 mg; Calcium 44 mg

Take control of home food safety. Be sure to keep raw meats or fish and ready-to-eat foods, such as salad greens or fresh vegetables, separate to avoid cross-contamination of bacteria. Use separate cutting boards for each and wash boards thoroughly with hot soapy water after each use.

Smoked Salmon Pizza with Red Onion and Dill

Dillweed is an herb that has been very popular in the Mediterranean area since the time of the Greeks. Both the feathery leaves and the fruits of the plant are used. Drying your own dillweed is much more economical than purchasing the herb commercially. Cut the fresh dillweed into small pieces with scissors and spread on a baking sheet covered with paper towels. Either dry at room temperature for a few days, stirring occasionally, or dry in the oven on a very low temperature, stirring occasionally. Store in a jar with a tight-fitting lid.

4 ounces cream cheese, softened
1/4 cup minced red onion
1 tablespoon chopped fresh dillweed
2 teaspoons grated lemon zest
1 teaspoon white horseradish
Salt and pepper to taste
1 (12-inch) pizza crust
4 ounces smoked salmon, thinly sliced

Beat the cream cheese, onion, dillweed, lemon zest and horseradish in a mixing bowl until mixed. Season with salt and pepper.

Spread the cream cheese mixture over the pizza crust. Arrange the salmon over the cream cheese mixture. Garnish with additional chopped fresh dillweed, sliced red onion and capers. Cut into 6 large slices for an entrée or into smaller portions and serve as an appetizer.

Serves 6

Nutrients Per Serving: Cal 225; Prot 11 g; Carbo 22 g; T Fat 10 g; (Saturated Fat 5 g); 40% Cal from Fat; Chol 29 mg; Fiber 1 g; Sod 685 mg; Calcium 27 mg

Poached Sole with Dill Sauce

1 (14-ounce) can chicken broth
6 (4-ounce) sole or flounder fillets
3 tablespoons lemon juice
1 tablespoon cornstarch
3 tablespoons fresh snipped dillweed, or 1 tablespoon dried dillweed
1 lemon, sliced (optional)

Bring 1¼ cups of the broth to a boil in a skillet over medium-high heat; reduce the heat. Add the sole. Simmer, covered, for 2 to 3 minutes or until the sole flakes easily with a fork. Remove the sole to a heated serving platter using a slotted spoon.

Combine the remaining broth, lemon juice and cornstarch in a small saucepan and mix well. Cook over medium-high heat until the mixture thickens and comes to a boil, stirring constantly. Boil for 1 minute. Stir in the dillweed. Spoon the sauce over the sole. Garnish with the lemon slices.

To prepare in the microwave, place the sole in a 2-quart microwave-safe dish. Pour 1¼ cups of the broth over the top. Microwave, covered with plastic wrap, on High for 5 to 6 minutes or until the sole flakes easily. Remove the sole to a heated platter.

Combine ¼ cup of the remaining broth, lemon juice and 2 tablespoons cornstarch in a 1-quart microwave dish and mix well. Microwave on High for 4 to 5 minutes or until the sauce thickens and comes to a boil. Stir in the dillweed. Spoon the sauce over the sole.

Serves 6

Nutrients Per Serving: Cal 110; Prot 20 g; Carbo 2 g; T Fat 2 g; (Saturated Fat <1 g); 14% Cal from Fat; Chol 53 mg; Fiber <1 g; Sod 294 mg; Calcium 20 mg

Fish is usually cooked by dry heat methods— broiling, baking, or frying—but moist heat methods such as poaching and steaming retain the delicate flavors and moistness of finfish and are time-efficient. Serve Poached Sole with Dill Sauce with Spinach and Strawberry Salad, on page 47, and Rich Muffins, on page 174, for a quick and delicious weeknight dinner.

Baked Tilapia with Lime Sauce

Aquaculture, or fish farming, is one of Maryland's fastest growing industries. Aquaculture products are in high demand because of their quality and year-round availability. Tilapia is the only Maryland fish raised exclusively in aquaculture. It is a white-fleshed fish with a mild flavor. The Lime Sauce in this recipe is a perfect accompaniment.

Lime Sauce
1/4 cup (1/2 stick) margarine
1 tablespoon flour
1/2 cup dry white wine
1/4 cup lime juice
3 green onions, chopped
1 large garlic clove, minced

Tilapia
4 (4-ounce) tilapia fillets
Salt and pepper to taste

For the sauce, heat the margarine in a saucepan. Add the flour and stir until blended. Stir in the wine, lime juice, green onions and garlic. Cook until reduced by 1/2, stirring frequently.

For the tilapia, arrange the fillets in a baking dish. Sprinkle with salt and pepper. Pour the sauce over the fillets. Bake at 450 degrees for 10 minutes per inch of thickness or until the fish flakes easily with a fork.

Serves 4

Nutrients Per Serving: Cal 212; Prot 18 g; Carbo 4 g; T Fat 12 g; (Saturated Fat 3 g); 51% Cal from Fat; Chol 44 mg; Fiber <1 g; Sod 169 mg; Calcium 26 mg

Grilled Tuna with Ginger Mango Salsa

Ginger Mango Salsa

2 cups chopped fresh mangoes
Sections of 1 orange, chopped
2 tablespoons chopped fresh
    cilantro
1 tablespoon chopped Vidalia or
    red onion
1 tablespoon grated orange
    zest
1/2 teaspoon ginger powder
1/4 teaspoon cumin
1/4 teaspoon Old Bay seasoning
1/8 teaspoon red pepper

Tuna

2 pounds fresh tuna
1/4 cup olive oil
1/4 cup tequila
1/4 cup lime juice
1 tablespoon Old Bay seasoning
1/2 teaspoon chopped fresh
    cilantro

For the salsa, combine the mangoes, orange, cilantro, onion, orange zest, ginger powder, cumin, Old Bay seasoning and red pepper in a bowl and mix gently.

For the tuna, place the tuna in a large sealable plastic bag. Combine the olive oil, tequila, lime juice, Old Bay seasoning and cilantro in a bowl and mix well. Pour the olive oil mixture over the tuna and seal tightly. Turn to coat.

Marinate in the refrigerator for 20 to 30 minutes, turning once or twice. Drain, reserving the marinade. Grill the tuna over hot coals for 5 minutes per side or until the tuna flakes easily with a fork, basting once after turning with the reserved marinade. Serve with the salsa.

Serves 4

Nutrients Per Serving: Cal 533; Prot 56 g; Carbo 34 g; T Fat 16 g; (Saturated Fat 2 g); 27% Cal from Fat; Chol 105 mg; Fiber 4 g; Sod 625 mg; Calcium 73 mg
Nutritional profile includes all the marinade.

The "fattier" varieties of fish such as mackerel, herring, bluefin tuna, and salmon contain a significant amount of omega-3 fatty acids. These special fats can keep the heart healthy by lowering blood cholesterol and preventing blood platelets from blocking arteries. Omega-3 fatty acids may also play a preventative role in arthritis, diabetes, and multiple sclerosis.

A Tuna Experience

Prepare a Tuna Experience in advance, pack a picnic cooler, and take a day trip. Consider visiting Annapolis, Maryland's state capital and a city of tradition. Annapolis has more surviving colonial buildings than any other place in the nation. Even the layout of the streets is a history lesson where State and Church Circles provide a visual reminder of the separation of church and state. While you are there, visit the U.S. Naval Academy, where a brigade of 4,000 men and women prepare for leadership roles in the Navy and Marine Corps.

2 (7-ounce) cans albacore tuna, drained, flaked
1/3 cup minced celery
2 tablespoons chopped sweet pickles
1 teaspoon minced onion
1/3 cup mayonnaise
1 teaspoon Dijon mustard
1/2 teaspoon lemon juice
1 (8- to 10-inch) loaf French or Italian bread
2 to 3 tablespoons olive oil
6 slices provolone cheese
Shredded lettuce to taste
Sliced tomatoes to taste

Combine the tuna, celery, pickles and onion in a bowl and mix well. Stir in the mayonnaise, Dijon mustard and lemon juice.

Slice the bread loaf horizontally into halves. If the loaf is thick, remove the center to create a shell for the filling. Drizzle the olive oil over the cut sides. Spread with the tuna filling. Top with the cheese, lettuce and tomatoes. The sandwiches may be heated in a 350-degree oven just long enough to crisp the bread if desired.

Serves 4

Nutrients Per Serving: Cal 524; Prot 37 g; Carbo 8 g; T Fat 37 g; (Saturated Fat 11 g); 65% Cal from Fat; Chol 72 mg; Fiber <1 g; Sod 957 mg; Calcium 346 mg

Reinhardt's Hard Fried Crabs

3 live crabs
1 or 2 eggs
Flour
Bread crumbs
Salt and pepper to taste
Vegetable oil for frying

Remove the shells, claws, aprons, devil and eyes from the crabs. Collect the brown fat from inside the shell and center of the crab body; strain.

Combine the reserved brown fat and eggs in a bowl and mix well. Add enough flour and bread crumbs to the egg mixture to form a stiff batter. Season with salt and pepper. Fill the crab cavity with the batter; a small portion may spill out over the shell.

Place the crab cavity side down in hot oil in a skillet. Fry until the fat forms a crisp coating but is soft inside; turn. Fry until the bits of batter that leaked out are brown.

Serves 1

Nutritional profile is not available for this recipe.

Popular crab feast condiments and side dishes include the following: vinegar and melted butter for dipping; sliced tomatoes; sweet corn on the cob; assorted salads, such as potato salad, coleslaw, or marinated vegetables; and watermelon.

Chesapeake Bay Soft-Shell Crabs

12 Maryland soft-shell crabs, cleaned
Salt and pepper to taste
Flour (optional)
Margarine, butter or vegetable oil for frying

Pat the crabs dry with paper towels. Sprinkle with salt and pepper. Lightly coat the crabs with flour.

Heat just enough margarine in a skillet to prevent the crabs from sticking. Fry the crabs in the margarine for 5 minutes per side; drain. The crabs may be deep-fried at 375 degrees for 2 to 3 minutes or until brown on all sides.

Serves 6

Nutrients Per Serving: Cal 279; Prot 57 g; Carbo 2 g; T Fat 3 g; (Saturated Fat <1 g); 11% Cal from Fat; Chol 193 mg; Fiber 0 g; Sod 960 mg; Calcium 150 mg
Nutritional profile does not include margarine, butter or oil for frying.

Fried Soft-Shell Crabs

1 cup flour
1 teaspoon salt
1 teaspoon pepper
1/2 teaspoon baking powder
12 Maryland soft-shell crabs, cleaned
Shortening or vegetable oil for frying

Combine the flour, salt, pepper and baking powder in a shallow dish and mix well. Coat the crabs with the flour mixture.

Heat enough shortening in a skillet or electric skillet to measure 1/2 inch. Heat to 375 degrees. Add the crabs to the hot shortening. Reduce the temperature to 350 degrees. Fry for 5 minutes per side or until brown; drain.

Makes 6 (2-crab) servings

Nutrients Per Serving: Cal 355; Prot 59 g; Carbo 18 g; T Fat 3 g; (Saturated Fat <1 g); 9% Cal from Fat; Chol 193 mg; Fiber 1 g; Sod 1388 mg; Calcium 176 mg
Nutritional profile does not include shortening or vegetable oil for frying.

Maryland Crab Cakes

1 cup seasoned bread crumbs
1/4 cup mayonnaise
1 egg, beaten
1 teaspoon Worcestershire sauce
1 teaspoon dry mustard
1/2 teaspoon salt
1/4 teaspoon pepper
1 pound crab meat, shells and cartilage removed
Margarine or butter for frying

Combine the bread crumbs, mayonnaise, egg, Worcestershire sauce, dry mustard, salt and pepper in a bowl and mix well. Add the crab meat and mix gently to combine.

Shape the crab meat mixture into 6 cakes. Heat just enough margarine in a skillet to prevent the cakes from sticking. Fry the cakes in the margarine for 5 minutes per side or until light brown; drain.

Makes 6 crab cakes

Nutrients Per Serving: Cal 158; Prot 4 g; Carbo 14 g; T Fat 9 g; (Saturated Fat 2 g);
51% Cal from Fat; Chol 44 mg; Fiber 1 g; Sod 800 mg; Calcium 28 mg
Nutritional profile does not include margarine or butter for frying.

Eastern Shore Crab Cakes

1 egg, lightly beaten
2 tablespoons mayonnaise
1 tablespoon prepared yellow mustard
1 tablespoon Worcestershire sauce
1 tablespoon seasoned bread crumbs
1 teaspoon Old Bay seasoning
1 teaspoon basil
1 pound lump or backfin crab meat, shells and cartilage removed
Parsley flakes (optional)

Combine the egg, mayonnaise, prepared mustard, Worcestershire sauce, bread crumbs, Old Bay seasoning and basil in a bowl and mix well. Add the crab meat and mix gently to combine.

Shape the crab meat mixture into 4 cakes. Arrange the cakes on a baking sheet. Sprinkle with parsley flakes. Bake at 350 degrees for 20 to 30 minutes or until brown. You may add additional mayonnaise and additional bread crumbs for the desired consistency and more Old Bay seasoning for a spicier crab cake. Substitute cracker crumbs for the bread crumbs if desired.

Makes 4 crab cakes

Nutrients Per Serving: Cal 85; Prot 3 g; Carbo 2 g; T Fat 7 g; (Saturated Fat 1 g); 76% Cal from Fat; Chol 61 mg; Fiber <1 g; Sod 368 mg; Calcium 19 mg

Crab Imperial

1/2 cup mayonnaise
1 egg, beaten
2 tablespoons whole or low-fat milk
1 teaspoon Old Bay seasoning
1/4 teaspoon pepper
1/4 teaspoon Worcestershire sauce
1 pound lump crab meat, shells and cartilage removed
Grated Parmesan cheese to taste

Combine the mayonnaise, egg, milk, Old Bay seasoning, pepper and Worcestershire sauce in a bowl and mix well. Add the crab meat and mix gently to combine.

Spray 5 baking shells or custard cups with nonstick cooking spray. Fill the shells with the crab mixture. Sprinkle with the cheese.

Arrange the shells on a baking sheet. Bake at 350 degrees for 25 to 30 minutes or until light brown. You may substitute lite mayonnaise for the regular mayonnaise.

Serves 5

Nutrients Per Serving: Cal 182; Prot 2 g; Carbo <1 g; T Fat 19 g; (Saturated Fat 4 g); 95% Cal from Fat; Chol 62 mg; Fiber 0 g; Sod 278 mg; Calcium 15 mg

Crab Imperial can be portioned into smaller quantities and served as an appetizer. Or dressed up for the main entrée and stuffed in a delicious portobello mushroom or your favorite white fish.

Crab Quiche

Having friends for a special luncheon? Serve this delightful quiche made from Maryland blue crab meat. Use a vase of Black-eyed Susans, the Maryland state flower, to create a beautiful centerpiece.

1/4 cup shortening
1 cup flour
5 tablespoons ice water
10 ounces backfin or lump crab meat or spinach
1 1/2 cups (6 ounces) chopped Swiss cheese
3 eggs, or equivalent amount of egg substitute
1 (12-ounce) can evaporated skim milk
2 tablespoons finely chopped onion
Pepper to taste
Nutmeg to taste
Tabasco sauce to taste

Cut the shortening into the flour in a bowl until crumbly. Add the ice water and mix until the mixture forms a ball. Roll the pastry between 2 sheets of plastic wrap. Fit the pastry into a 9-inch pie plate; crimp the edges.

Sprinkle the crab meat in the pastry-lined pie plate. Top with the cheese. Whisk the eggs in a bowl until blended. Stir in the evaporated skim milk. Add the onion, pepper, nutmeg and Tabasco sauce and mix well.

Pour the egg mixture into the prepared pie plate. Bake at 375 degrees for 40 minutes or until light brown and set. Let stand for 10 minutes before serving. Cut into 8 wedges and serve immediately.

Serves 8

Nutrients Per Serving: Cal 272; Prot 15 g; Carbo 18 g; T Fat 16 g; (Saturated Fat 7 g); 52% Cal from Fat; Chol 107 mg; Fiber <1 g; Sod 146 mg; Calcium 376 mg

Eastern Shore Oyster Fritters

1 pint shucked Maryland standard oysters
1 cup baking mix
2 tablespoons cornmeal
1 teaspoon salt
1/4 teaspoon pepper
1/2 cup evaporated milk
3/4 cup vegetable oil

Drain the oysters, reserving the liquor. Combine the baking mix, cornmeal, salt and pepper in a bowl and mix well. Stir in the evaporated milk. Fold in the oysters; the batter will be thick.

Heat the oil in a 10-inch skillet. Drop the batter by tablespoonfuls into the hot oil; each fritter should contain 2 oysters. Fry for 1 to 2 minutes or until brown on 1 side; turn carefully. Fry until brown; drain. If the consistency of the batter becomes too thick on standing, thin with some of the reserved oyster liquor.

Makes 18 fritters

Nutrients Per Serving: Cal 138; Prot 3 g; Carbo 9 g; T Fat 10 g; (Saturated Fat 2 g);
66% Cal from Fat; Chol 14 mg; Fiber 1 g; Sod 254 mg; Calcium 39 mg
Nutritional profile includes the vegetable oil.

Conservation laws passed to protect the Bay's oyster population state that only sail-powered vessels can dredge for oysters. In response to this law, Skipjacks were developed. They are the last working sailboats in the country.

Grilled Scallops with Black Beans

1 pound sea scallops
1 teaspoon olive oil
1/2 teaspoon cumin
1/4 teaspoon red pepper
1 cup chopped onion
2 teaspoons minced garlic
1/2 cup minced red bell pepper
2 cups drained canned black beans, rinsed
1 teaspoon balsamic vinegar

Place the scallops in a single layer in a shallow glass or plastic dish. Combine the olive oil, cumin and red pepper in a small bowl and mix well. Drizzle the olive oil mixture over the scallops. Marinate, covered, in the refrigerator for 30 minutes, stirring occasionally.

Spray a large nonstick skillet with nonstick cooking spray. Heat over medium-high heat. Sauté the onion and garlic in the hot skillet until the onion is tender. Stir in the bell pepper. Sauté until the bell pepper is tender. Add the beans and mix well.

Cook until heated through, stirring frequently. Remove from heat. Stir in the vinegar. Cover to keep warm. Grill the scallops over hot coals until opaque. Arrange the scallops over the bean mixture on a serving platter. Serve immediately.

Serves 4

Nutrients Per Serving: Cal 197; Prot 16 g; Carbo 25 g; T Fat 3 g; (Saturated Fat <1 g); 14% Cal from Fat; Chol 18 mg; Fiber 6 g; Sod 508 mg; Calcium 65 mg

Vegetables & Side Dishes

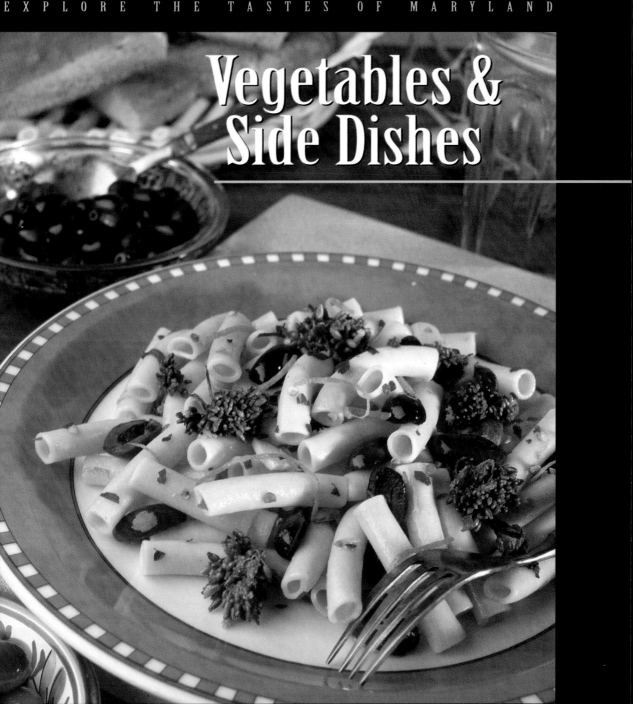

Vegetables & Side Dishes

Country Lima Beans

8 ounces dried lima beans
1 small onion, cut into 1/4-inch slices
1/2 cup ketchup
2 tablespoons light molasses
1 tablespoon brown sugar
1 tablespoon chili sauce
1 teaspoon salt
1/2 teaspoon dry mustard
4 slices bacon, crisp-cooked, crumbled (optional)

Sort and rinse the beans. Combine the beans with enough water to cover in a saucepan. Bring to a boil. Boil for 2 minutes. Remove from heat. Let stand, covered, for 1 hour.

Add enough additional water to the beans to cover if needed. Bring to a boil; reduce the heat. Simmer for 30 minutes or until tender, stirring occasionally. Do not boil as boiling will cause the beans to burst. Drain, reserving the liquid.

Layer the beans and onion in an ungreased 11/2-quart baking dish. Mix the ketchup, molasses, brown sugar, chili sauce, salt and dry mustard in a bowl. Spoon the ketchup mixture over the prepared layers. Add enough of the reserved liquid to cover.

Bake, covered, at 300 degrees for 1 hour. Stir in the bacon.

Serves 7

Nutrients Per Serving: Cal 156; Prot 7 g; Carbo 32 g; T Fat <1 g; (Saturated Fat <1 g); 3% Cal from Fat; Chol 0 mg; Fiber 7 g; Sod 574 mg; Calcium 44 mg

A great alternative to traditional baked beans. After cooking, transfer to a slow cooker for serving at your next cookout!

Italian Green Beans

1 cup chopped onion
2 tablespoons butter or olive oil
3 (14-ounce) cans whole tomatoes
3 (16-ounce) cans cut green beans, drained
3/4 teaspoon oregano
3/4 teaspoon basil
1/4 teaspoon salt
1/4 teaspoon pepper

Sauté the onion in the butter in a saucepan until tender. Drain the tomatoes, reserving the juice. Cut the tomatoes into quarters.

Add the reserved juice, tomatoes, beans, oregano, basil, salt and pepper to the onion and mix well. Simmer for 15 minutes or until heated through, stirring occasionally. You may substitute 6 cups lightly steamed fresh green beans for the canned green beans.

Makes 10 (1/2-cup) servings

Nutrients Per Serving: Cal 72; Prot 2 g; Carbo 11 g; T Fat 2 g; (Saturated Fat 1 g); 29% Cal from Fat; Chol 6 mg; Fiber 4 g; Sod 697 mg; Calcium 62 mg

Don't just think of fresh green beans as a side vegetable. Blanch and chill the beans and add to salads or serve on vegetable trays with your favorite dips.

Carrot Soufflé

Soufflé

2 (14-ounce) cans sliced
    carrots, drained
1 cup (2 sticks) butter or lite
    margarine, melted
1 cup sugar
6 eggs, or 12 egg whites
6 tablespoons flour
2 teaspoons baking powder
1 teaspoon vanilla extract
1/4 teaspoon cinnamon
1/4 teaspoon nutmeg

Topping

1 cup cornflakes or Special-K
1/4 cup walnuts, chopped
2 tablespoons brown sugar
1/4 teaspoon cinnamon
1/4 teaspoon nutmeg
2 tablespoons butter or lite
    margarine, melted

This is a delicious vegetable side dish to serve at Thanksgiving or Christmas. It is often mistaken for sweet potatoes. For a more heart-healthy version, try substituting 12 egg whites or 1 1/2 cups egg substitute for the whole eggs and lite margarine for the butter.

For the soufflé, combine the carrots, butter, sugar, eggs, flour, baking powder, vanilla, cinnamon and nutmeg in a blender. Process until smooth. Pour the carrot mixture into a 3-quart round microwave-safe baking dish or a microwave-safe 9×13-inch baking dish sprayed with nonstick cooking spray.

For the topping, combine the cereal, walnuts, brown sugar, cinnamon and nutmeg in a bowl and mix well. Add the butter and toss until coated. Spread the cereal mixture over the prepared layer. Bake at 350 degrees for 45 minutes or until the edge of the soufflé is cooked through. Microwave on High for 10 to 15 minutes or until a knife inserted in the center comes out clean.

Serves 12

Nutrients Per Serving: Cal 319; Prot 4 g; Carbo 29 g; T Fat 21 g; (Saturated Fat 12 g); 59% Cal from Fat; Chol 153 mg; Fiber 2 g; Sod 476 mg; Calcium 78 mg

Corn Pudding

2 cups cream-style corn
2 tablespoons flour
1 cup low-fat milk
3 tablespoons reduced-fat margarine, melted
1 tablespoon sugar
1 teaspoon salt
3 eggs, beaten

Combine the corn and flour in a bowl and mix well. Stir in the low-fat milk, margarine, sugar and salt. Add the eggs and stir until mixed.

Spoon the corn mixture into a $1^{1}/_{2}$-quart baking dish sprayed with nonstick cooking spray. Place the baking dish in a larger baking pan. Add enough hot water to the baking pan to reach halfway up the side of the baking dish. Bake at 325 degrees for $1^{1}/_{2}$ hours or until set.

Makes 4 ($^{1}/_{2}$-cup) servings

Nutrients Per Serving: Cal 250; Prot 9 g; Carbo 33 g; T Fat 11 g; (Saturated Fat 3 g); 37% Cal from Fat; Chol 164 mg; Fiber 2 g; Sod 1121 mg; Calcium 97 mg

Dishes similar to this Corn Pudding were no doubt served for the likes of Charles Mason and Jeremiah Dixon. Mason and Dixon, English astronomers and mathematicians, were commissioned in 1763 to complete a land survey and settle a dispute between William Penn and Frederick Calvert. The resultant Mason-Dixon Line defined the boundary between Maryland and Pennsylvania. Today, it is considered a landmark in the history of geodesy, the science of determining positions on large portions of the earth.

Northern-Style Corn Fritters

2 cups fresh corn kernels
2 egg yolks
2 tablespoons flour
2 teaspoons sugar (optional)
1/2 teaspoon salt
1/4 teaspoon pepper
2 egg whites
1/2 cup shortening

Place the corn in a bowl. Scrape the corn cobs, releasing the milk into the bowl containing the corn. Whisk the egg yolks in a small bowl until blended. Add the egg yolks to the corn and mix well. Stir in the flour, sugar, salt and pepper. Beat the egg whites in a mixing bowl until stiff peaks form. Fold the egg whites into the corn mixture.

Heat the shortening in a skillet to 350 degrees. Drop the corn mixture by tablespoonfuls into the hot shortening. Cook until brown on both sides, turning once; drain. Serve as a side dish or for breakfast or brunch with butter and syrup. You may cook the fritters on a griddle with a small amount of shortening.

Makes 6 (3-fritter) servings

Nutrients Per Serving: Cal 230; Prot 4 g; Carbo 12 g; T Fat 19 g; (Saturated Fat 5 g);
73% Cal from Fat; Chol 71 mg; Fiber 1 g; Sod 222 mg; Calcium 10 mg
Nutritional profile includes all of the shortening.

Bittersweet Onions

1 pound onions, cut into halves
1 (8-ounce) can tomato juice or tomato sauce
1/2 cup water
1 beef bouillon cube
1/4 cup packed brown sugar
1 tablespoon lemon juice
1 teaspoon prepared mustard (optional)
1/2 teaspoon Worcestershire sauce (optional)
1/4 teaspoon Mrs. Dash seasoning
1/8 teaspoon salt (optional)

Arrange the onions in a single layer in a baking dish. Heat the tomato juice, water and bouillon cube in a saucepan until the bouillon dissolves, stirring occasionally. Add the brown sugar, lemon juice, prepared mustard, Worcestershire sauce, Mrs. Dash seasoning and salt and mix well.

Cook until the brown sugar dissolves, stirring occasionally. Pour the tomato juice mixture over the onions. Bake at 350 degrees for 50 minutes or until the onions are tender.

Makes 4 (1/2-cup) servings

Nutrients Per Serving: Cal 107; Prot 2 g; Carbo 26 g; T Fat <1 g; (Saturated Fat <1 g); 2% Cal from Fat; Chol <1 mg; Fiber 2 g; Sod 429 mg; Calcium 40 mg

Early June Peas with Honeyed Pecans

1 (16-ounce) package frozen early June peas
1 tablespoon butter
3 tablespoons coarsely chopped pecans
1 tablespoon honey

Prepare the peas using package directions; drain. Cover to keep warm. Heat the butter in a small saucepan until melted. Stir in the pecans and honey. Pour the honey mixture over the peas and stir until coated.

Makes 5 (1/2-cup) servings

Nutrients Per Serving: Cal 132; Prot 5 g; Carbo 17 g; T Fat 6 g; (Saturated Fat 2 g); 39% Cal from Fat; Chol 6 mg; Fiber 5 g; Sod 194 mg; Calcium 4 mg

Ever wonder why you cry when you chop onions? Onions have unstable sulfur compounds that are released when onions are cut and thus cause tears. There is a theory that most of the compounds are stored in the root end of the onion, which may explain why chopping that part last helps to minimize watery eyes!

Basil Potato Mix

1 pound white potatoes
1 pound sweet potatoes
2 tablespoons olive oil
2 tablespoons minced garlic
2 tablespoons basil leaves
1/2 teaspoon salt, or to taste

Cook the white potatoes and sweet potatoes in boiling water in separate saucepans for 15 to 20 minutes or until tender; drain. Let stand until cool. Peel the potatoes and cut into 2-inch pieces. Heat the olive oil in a skillet over medium heat. Add the potatoes and garlic. Sauté for 5 to 10 minutes or until the potatoes are brown. Stir in the basil and salt. Serve immediately.

Makes 8 (1/2-cup) servings

Nutrients Per Serving: Cal 139; Prot 2 g; Carbo 25 g; T Fat 4 g; (Saturated Fat 1 g); 23% Cal from Fat; Chol 0 mg; Fiber 2 g; Sod 155 mg; Calcium 16 mg

Microwave Scalloped Potatoes

3 tablespoons margarine, melted
2 tablespoons flour
1 teaspoon salt
1/4 teaspoon pepper
2 cups milk
3 1/2 to 4 cups thinly sliced potatoes
2 tablespoons minced onion

Combine the margarine, flour, salt and pepper in a microwave-safe bowl and mix well. Add the milk gradually, stirring constantly until blended. Microwave on High for 8 to 10 minutes, stirring every 4 minutes. Layer the potatoes, onion and milk mixture in a 2-quart microwave-safe dish until all of the ingredients are used, ending with the milk mixture. Microwave on High for 17 to 19 minutes or until the potatoes are tender. Let stand for 5 minutes before serving.

Serves 8

Nutrients Per Serving: Cal 168; Prot 4 g; Carbo 24 g; T Fat 6 g; (Saturated Fat 2 g); 34% Cal from Fat; Chol 8 mg; Fiber 2 g; Sod 377 mg; Calcium 83 mg

You may also want to try fresh basil in a salad. Fresh basil will stay aromatic and green at room temperature for weeks when placed in a glass of water. Be sure to change the water daily. If you grow basil in your garden, transfer some of the plants in the fall and grow inside in a sunny window. Fresh basil will then be at your fingertips during most of the winter.

Stewed Potatoes

4 cups water
1/2 cup chopped cooked ham or beef
6 medium potatoes, peeled, coarsely chopped
1 medium yellow onion, coarsely chopped
Salt and pepper to taste

Combine the water and ham in a 2-quart saucepan. Bring to a boil; reduce the heat. Simmer for 15 minutes, stirring occasionally. Add the potatoes and onion, mixing well and adding additional water if needed to cover the potatoes. Season with salt and pepper.

Cook over low heat until the potatoes are tender and the liquid is the consistency of gravy, stirring occasionally.

Makes 4 (1/2-cup) servings

Nutrients Per Serving: Cal 298; Prot 12 g; Carbo 60 g; T Fat 2 g; (Saturated Fat 1 g); 6% Cal from Fat; Chol 16 mg; Fiber 6 g; Sod 31 mg; Calcium 29 mg

Superb Butternut Squash

2 cups mashed cooked peeled butternut squash
1/2 cup sugar
1/3 cup orange juice
1/3 cup nonfat dry milk powder
2 eggs, beaten
2 tablespoons melted butter
1/2 teaspoon salt
1/2 cup golden or dark raisins or cranraisins

Combine the squash, sugar, orange juice, milk powder, eggs, butter and salt in a bowl and mix well. Stir in the raisins. Spoon the squash mixture into a greased 1 1/2-quart baking dish. Bake at 350 degrees for 60 to 65 minutes or until set. Decrease the preparation time by purchasing the squash already cooked in the frozen section of the supermarket.

Serves 6

Nutrients Per Serving: Cal 212; Prot 5 g; Carbo 38 g; T Fat 6 g; (Saturated Fat 3 g); 23% Cal from Fat; Chol 81 mg; Fiber 3 g; Sod 282 mg; Calcium 105 mg

Twice-Baked Squash

2 (1¼- to 1½-pound) acorn squash
Salt to taste
1½ cups sliced celery
¼ cup chopped onion
1 (4-ounce) can diced green chiles, drained
1 tablespoon cumin seeds, ground
½ teaspoon garlic salt
⅛ teaspoon pepper
2 tablespoons margarine
1 (10-ounce) package frozen whole kernel corn, thawed, drained
2 tablespoons sunflower seeds
1 whole pimiento, cut into diamond shapes (optional)

Cut the squash into halves and remove the seeds. Arrange the halves cut side down in a shallow baking pan. Bake at 350 degrees for 30 minutes. Turn the squash and sprinkle the cut sides with salt. Bake for 20 to 30 minutes longer or until tender. Cool slightly.

Scoop out the squash pulp carefully, leaving a ¼- to ½-inch shell. Place the squash pulp in a bowl and mash. Sauté the celery, onion, green chiles, cumin, garlic salt and pepper in the margarine in a skillet until the celery and onion are tender. Add the sautéed mixture to the mashed squash and mix well. Stir in the corn and sunflower seeds.

Arrange the squash shells in a shallow baking dish. Spoon the squash mixture evenly into the shells. Bake at 350 degrees for 25 to 30 minutes or until heated through. Garnish with the pimiento.

Serves 4

Nutrients Per Serving: Cal 269; Prot 6 g; Carbo 48 g; T Fat 9 g; (Saturated Fat 2 g); 28% Cal from Fat; Chol 0 mg; Fiber 8 g; Sod 680 mg; Calcium 133 mg

Summer Squash and Spinach Bake

2 pounds yellow squash, sliced
1/2 cup chopped onion
1 cup water
2 cups fresh spinach, chopped
1/2 cup (2 ounces) shredded Cheddar cheese
1/2 cup vanilla yogurt
1 egg, beaten
1/4 teaspoon pepper
1/2 cup cracker crumbs

Combine the squash, onion and water in a saucepan. Bring to a boil; reduce the heat. Simmer for 5 to 10 minutes or until the squash is tender; drain.

Mash the squash mixture in a bowl. Stir in the spinach. Add the cheese, yogurt, egg and pepper and mix well. Spoon the squash mixture into a lightly greased 2-quart baking dish. Sprinkle with the cracker crumbs. Bake at 350 degrees for 40 minutes or until set.

Serves 6

Nutrients Per Serving: Cal 134; Prot 7 g; Carbo 15 g; T Fat 6 g; (Saturated Fat 3 g); 36% Cal from Fat; Chol 47 mg; Fiber 4 g; Sod 169 mg; Calcium 156 mg

Squash comes in two main varieties: summer and winter. Summer squash includes zucchini, yellow crookneck, and pattypan squash. Winter squash includes butternut and Hubbard. Both types of squash are considered good sources of potassium.

Zucchini Casserole

2 pounds zucchini, sliced
1/4 cup chopped onion
1 (10-ounce) can cream of chicken soup
1 cup low-fat sour cream
1 cup shredded carrots
1 (8-ounce) package herb-seasoned stuffing mix
1 cup (2 sticks) low-fat margarine, melted

Add the zucchini and onion to boiling water in a saucepan. Boil for 5 minutes; do not overcook. Drain in a colander.

Combine the soup and sour cream in a bowl and mix well. Stir in the carrots. Fold in the squash mixture. Toss the stuffing mix and margarine in a bowl until coated. Spread 1/2 of the stuffing mixture in a 9×13-inch baking dish. Spread with the squash mixture and sprinkle with the remaining stuffing mixture. Bake at 350 degrees for 25 to 30 minutes or until brown and bubbly.

Serves 8

Nutrients Per Serving: Cal 331; Prot 8 g; Carbo 32 g; T Fat 20 g; (Saturated Fat 6 g); 53% Cal from Fat; Chol 13 mg; Fiber 4 g; Sod 983 mg; Calcium 98 mg

Old Bay Zucchini and Tomatoes

3 medium zucchini, sliced
1/2 medium onion, chopped
1 1/2 tablespoons olive oil
2 tomatoes, seeded,
   chopped
1 teaspoon Old Bay seasoning
1/4 teaspoon freshly ground
   pepper
1/2 cup (2 ounces) shredded
   mozzarella cheese

Sauté the zucchini and onion in the olive oil in a skillet for a few minutes. Stir in the tomatoes, Old Bay seasoning and pepper. Reduce the heat to low.

Simmer, covered, for 5 minutes, stirring occasionally. Sprinkle with the cheese. Simmer, covered, for 5 minutes longer.

Makes 4 (1-cup) servings

Nutrients Per Serving: Cal 123; Prot 5 g; Carbo 9 g; T Fat 9 g; (Saturated Fat 3 g); 58% Cal from Fat; Chol 11 mg; Fiber 3 g; Sod 228 mg; Calcium 100 mg

Ahh. . . the summer tomato! Besides being a culinary delight, tomatoes contain a phytochemical called lycopene that helps to give them their red color. Scientists are studying tomatoes and lycopene because they seem to offer protection against cancers of the esophagus, prostate, and stomach. Watermelon and pink grapefruit also contain lycopene.

Baked Tomatoes

6 medium tomatoes
1/2 cup soft bread crumbs
1/4 cup grated Parmesan
    cheese
2 tablespoons fresh snipped
    parsley
1 teaspoon sugar
1/4 teaspoon pepper

1/4 teaspoon basil
1/4 teaspoon dillweed
1/8 teaspoon thyme
1/8 teaspoon oregano
1/8 teaspoon salt
1/8 teaspoon garlic powder
2 tablespoons butter

Cut the tomatoes into halves. Arrange the tomato halves cut side up in a baking dish. Combine the bread crumbs, cheese, parsley, sugar, pepper, basil, dillweed, thyme, oregano, salt and garlic powder in a bowl and mix well.

Spoon some of the bread crumb mixture on each tomato half. Top each with 1/2 teaspoon butter. Bake at 350 degrees for 25 minutes.

Serves 12

Nutrients Per Serving: Cal 44; Prot 1 g; Carbo 4 g; T Fat 3 g; (Saturated Fat 2 g); 52% Cal from Fat; Chol 7 mg; Fiber 1 g; Sod 91 mg; Calcium 29 mg

Marinated Summer Tomatoes

3 medium tomatoes, sliced
1 medium cucumber, peeled, sliced
1 medium green bell pepper, cut into 1-inch pieces
6 tablespoons water
6 tablespoons olive oil
1/4 cup sugar
1/4 cup white vinegar
2 tablespoons lemon juice

Arrange the tomatoes, cucumber and bell pepper on a glass serving platter or in a glass or plastic bowl. Whisk the water, olive oil, sugar, vinegar and lemon juice in a bowl until mixed. Drizzle the olive oil mixture over the vegetables. Marinate, covered, in the refrigerator for 2 to 10 hours. You may substitute 1 pint cherry tomato halves for the medium tomatoes.

Serves 6

Nutrients Per Serving: Cal 208; Prot 1 g; Carbo 22 g; T Fat 14 g; (Saturated Fat 2 g); 58% Cal from Fat; Chol <1 mg; Fiber 1 g; Sod 15 mg; Calcium 13 mg

Swiss Vegetable Medley

1 (16-ounce) package frozen broccoli, carrots and cauliflower, thawed, drained
1 (10-ounce) can cream of mushroom soup
1 cup (4 ounces) shredded Swiss cheese
1 (4-ounce) jar chopped pimientos, drained
1/3 cup sour cream
1 (2-ounce) can French-fried onions
1/4 teaspoon pepper

Combine the broccoli mixture, soup, 1/2 cup of the cheese, pimientos, sour cream, 1/2 of the onions and pepper in a bowl and mix gently. Spoon the broccoli mixture into a 1-quart baking dish. Bake, covered, at 350 degrees for 30 minutes; remove the cover. Sprinkle with the remaining 1/2 cup cheese and remaining onions. Bake for 5 minutes longer.

Serves 6

Nutrients Per Serving: Cal 233; Prot 9 g; Carbo 13 g; T Fat 16 g; (Saturated Fat 6 g); 62% Cal from Fat; Chol 23 mg; Fiber 3 g; Sod 567 mg; Calcium 218 mg

Is there a budding astronaut in your household? Prepare Marinated Summer Tomatoes early in the day so you and your aspiring astronaut can visit the NASA/Goddard Space Flight Center in Greenbelt. The visitor center and museum will fascinate future astronauts of all ages with close-up views of satellites, rockets, and space capsules. Serve with barbecued chicken basted with Southern Barbecue Sauce, on page 66, and Eastern Shore Corn Bread, on page 53. Working ahead of time makes serving a healthy dinner a snap.

Oven-Roasted Vegetables

1 large onion
3 tablespoons lite vinaigrette salad dressing
1 garlic clove, sliced
$1/2$ teaspoon rosemary, crushed
1 cup peeled whole baby carrots
3 medium red potatoes, cut into 1-inch pieces
$1/2$ large red bell pepper, cut into 1-inch pieces

Cut the onion lengthwise into halves, leaving the root intact. Cut 1 onion half into wedges, leaving the root attached to each wedge. Reserve the other onion half for another recipe.

Whisk the salad dressing, garlic and rosemary in a bowl. Add the onion, carrots, potatoes and bell pepper and mix until coated. Arrange the vegetables in a single layer on a baking sheet sprayed with nonstick cooking spray. Bake at 425 degrees for 40 to 50 minutes or until the vegetables are tender and light brown, turning once.

Serves 4

Nutrients Per Serving: Cal 129; Prot 4 g; Carbo 28 g; T Fat 3 g; (Saturated Fat <1 g); 15% Cal from Fat; Chol 0 mg; Fiber 4 g; Sod 102 mg; Calcium 32 mg

Barley Casserole

1 (16-ounce) can kidney beans, drained
1¹/₃ cups chicken broth
¹/₂ cup pearl barley
2 medium carrots, thinly sliced
1 small onion, chopped
2 tablespoons parsley flakes, or ¹/₄ cup chopped fresh parsley
¹/₄ teaspoon garlic powder
1 cup (4 ounces) shredded Cheddar cheese

Combine the beans, broth, pearl barley, carrots, onion, parsley flakes and garlic powder in a 1-quart baking dish and mix well. Bake, covered, at 350 degrees for 1 hour.

Sprinkle with the cheese. Bake until the cheese melts. Serve with crusty bread, tossed salad and fresh fruit.

Serves 4

Nutrients Per Serving: Cal 328; Prot 18 g; Carbo 42 g; T Fat 11 g; (Saturated Fat 6 g); 29% Cal from Fat; Chol 30 mg; Fiber 9 g; Sod 843 mg; Calcium 262 mg

Pearl barley is an ancient hardy grain used throughout the world. This type of barley has had the bran removed. Vitamins and minerals have been lost in the processing, but are added back. Whole grain barley is also sold, but pearl barley is the most common form used.

Apple Cheese Noodle Kugel

Kugel, Yiddish for "pudding," is a traditional Jewish dish. There are many different versions of noodle kugel, but this version is the contributor's favorite and is considered a comfort food for her.

8 ounces medium or wide egg noodles
2 tablespoons reduced-fat margarine
1 cup unsweetened applesauce
1 cup low-fat cottage cheese
1 egg, lightly beaten
1 egg white, lightly beaten
2 tablespoons sugar
1/4 teaspoon cinnamon

Cook the pasta using package directions; drain. Combine the pasta and margarine in a bowl and stir until the margarine melts. Stir in the applesauce. Add the cottage cheese, egg, egg white, sugar and cinnamon and mix gently.

Spoon the pasta mixture into a 2-quart baking dish sprayed with nonstick cooking spray. Bake at 350 degrees until golden and crusty.

Serves 6

Nutrients Per Serving: Cal 247; Prot 12 g; Carbo 37 g; T Fat 6 g; (Saturated Fat 2 g); 20% Cal from Fat; Chol 74 mg; Fiber 2 g; Sod 225 mg; Calcium 43 mg

Desserts

Desserts

Fruit and Nut Candy

1 cup dried apricots
1 cup raisins
1 cup dates
1 cup walnuts
1 cup shredded coconut
1 tablespoon lemon juice

Combine the apricots, raisins, dates, walnuts and coconut in a food grinder or food processor. Process until finely chopped. Stir in the lemon juice. Shape by tablespoonfuls into small balls and place in miniature cupcake liners or press the mixture into an 8×8-inch dish. Chill until firm and cut into squares. Or sprinkle the dried fruit mixture over hot cereal.

Makes 80 balls

Nutrients Per Serving: Cal 31; Prot <1 g; Carbo 5 g; T Fat 1 g; (Saturated Fat <1 g); 34% Cal from Fat; Chol 0 mg; Fiber <1 g; Sod 3 mg; Calcium 4 mg

Lickety-Split Granola

8 cups rolled oats
Chopped nuts (optional)
Sesame seeds (optional)
Chopped dried fruit (optional)
2/3 cup honey
1/2 cup vegetable oil
1/4 cup water
1/2 teaspoon cinnamon or allspice

Combine the oats, nuts, sesame seeds and dried fruit in a bowl and mix well. Mix the honey, oil, water and cinnamon in a small bowl. Add the honey mixture to the oats mixture and stir until coated. Spread the oats mixture on 2 baking sheets. Bake on the top oven rack at 300 degrees for 25 to 30 minutes or until golden brown, stirring halfway through the baking process. Let stand until cool. Store in a jar with a tight-fitting lid.

Makes 16 (1/2-cup) servings

Nutrients Per Serving: Cal 300; Prot 8 g; Carbo 46 g; T Fat 11 g; (Saturated Fat 2 g); 31% Cal from Fat; Chol 0 mg; Fiber 6 g; Sod 1 mg; Calcium 1 mg

Adding dried fruits to your diet is another way to help get "5-A-Day," or at least five servings of fruits and vegetables per day. Dried fruits have a long shelf life and are convenient. Because water is removed when drying fruits, all are concentrated sources of sugar and fiber. One and one-third ounces of a dried fruit is considered a serving. This is equal to about four to five prunes or two tablespoons of raisins.

Cinnamon-Poached Apples

Maryland orchards produce a variety of apples. For a snack or for use in salads try Empire, Jonathan, Golden Delicious, Red Delicious, or Gala. For cooking or baking try Jonathan, York, Rome, or McIntosh. If you are interested in visiting a Maryland orchard, check out their website at www.marylandapples.org.

6 medium Jonathan, McIntosh or Rome apples
3 cups apple cider or apple juice
1/3 cup sugar
1/4 cup red hot cinnamon candies
1 tablespoon sugar
1 tablespoon cornstarch
1/2 cup frozen whipped topping, thawed
Grated lemon zest to taste
Cinnamon to taste

Peel the apples and cut horizontally into halves; remove the cores. Combine the apple cider, 1/3 cup sugar and cinnamon candies in a saucepan. Cook until the sugar and candies dissolve, stirring frequently. Add the apples and mix gently. Bring to a boil; reduce the heat.

Simmer, covered, for 8 minutes or until the apples are tender, turning several times. Let stand until cool. Remove the apples to a bowl with a slotted spoon, reserving 1 1/2 cups of the liquid. Chill the apples for 2 hours.

Combine 1 tablespoon sugar and cornstarch in a saucepan and mix well. Add the reserved liquid and mix well. Cook over medium heat until thickened, stirring constantly. Let stand until cool.

To serve, place 2 apple halves cut side up on each dessert plate. Drizzle with the sauce. Top each serving with a dollop of whipped cream and sprinkle with the lemon zest and cinnamon.

Serves 6

Nutrients Per Serving: Cal 247; Prot <1 g; Carbo 60 g; T Fat 1 g; (Saturated Fat 1 g); 5% Cal from Fat; Chol 0 mg; Fiber 2 g; Sod 15 mg; Calcium 5 mg

Hot Fruit Compote

1 (20-ounce) can juice-pack pineapple chunks
4 bananas, sliced
1 (16-ounce) can juice-pack pears, drained, sliced
1 (16-ounce) can juice-pack peaches, drained, sliced
1 (16-ounce) can dark pitted sweet cherries, drained
1/2 cup packed brown sugar
1/2 cup (1 stick) margarine
1/4 cup sweet cream sherry
1/4 (16-ounce) package vanilla wafers, crushed
1/4 cup slivered almonds

Drain the pineapple, reserving the juice. Toss the bananas with the reserved juice in a bowl and drain. Add the pineapple, pears, peaches and cherries to the bananas and mix gently. Spoon the fruit mixture into a 9x13-inch baking dish.

Combine the brown sugar, margarine and sherry in a saucepan. Bring to a boil, stirring frequently. Pour the sherry mixture over the fruit. Sprinkle with the wafer crumbs and almonds. Bake at 350 degrees for 30 minutes. Serve warm.

Serves 12

Nutrients Per Serving: Cal 297; Prot 2 g; Carbo 52 g; T Fat 11 g; (Saturated Fat 2 g); 31% Cal from Fat; Chol 1 mg; Fiber 3 g; Sod 129 mg; Calcium 44 mg

Dress up a winter dinner party with this simple-to-prepare dessert. Friends will think you were in the kitchen for hours!

Peach Cobbler

1/2 cup (1 stick) butter
1 cup sugar
3/4 cup self-rising flour
1/2 teaspoon baking powder
1/8 teaspoon salt
3/4 cup milk
2 cups chopped fresh or canned peaches

Heat the butter in a 6×9-inch baking dish in a 350-degree oven until melted. Combine the sugar, self-rising flour, baking powder and salt in a bowl and mix well. Stir in the milk.

Pour the batter into the prepared baking dish; do not stir. Spoon the peaches in the center of the batter; do not stir. Bake at 350 degrees for 1 hour. Serve warm.

Makes 6 (1/2-cup) servings

Nutrients Per Serving: Cal 388; Prot 4 g; Carbo 59 g; T Fat 17 g; (Saturated Fat 10 g); 37% Cal from Fat; Chol 46 mg; Fiber 3 g; Sod 459 mg; Calcium 122 mg

Cobblers can be prepared with a variety of fruits. Try substituting fresh apples or berries for the peaches for a tasty summer dessert.

Cinnamon Apple Crisp

1 cup sugar
3/4 cup flour
1 teaspoon cinnamon
1/2 teaspoon salt
1/2 cup (1 stick) margarine
4 cups sliced peeled tart apples

Combine the sugar, flour, cinnamon and salt in a bowl and mix well. Cut in the margarine until crumbly.

Mound the apples in a 9-inch baking dish. Sprinkle the sugar mixture over the apples and pat lightly to the edge of the baking dish. Bake at 350 degrees for 45 minutes or until light brown and the apples are tender. Serve warm or at room temperature topped with ice cream or a wedge of Cheddar cheese.

You may prepare the crisp several hours in advance and store, covered, in the refrigerator. Bake just before serving. Or the sugar mixture may be mixed in advance and combined with the apples just before baking.

Serves 8

Nutrients Per Serving: Cal 272; Prot 1 g; Carbo 42 g; T Fat 12 g; (Saturated Fat 2 g); 38% Cal from Fat; Chol 0 mg; Fiber 1 g; Sod 279 mg; Calcium 9 mg

Cranberry Apple Crisp

1 (12-ounce) package fresh cranberries
2 large apples, thinly sliced
1/2 cup sugar
1/4 cup flour
1 teaspoon cinnamon
3/4 cup rolled oats
1/2 cup chopped walnuts (optional)
2 tablespoons brown sugar
3 tablespoons butter or margarine, melted

Combine the cranberries, apples, sugar, 1 tablespoon of the flour and cinnamon in a bowl and mix well. Spoon the cranberry mixture into a greased shallow 1 1/2-quart baking dish.

Combine the remaining flour, oats, walnuts and brown sugar in a bowl and mix well. Add the butter, stirring until crumbly. Sprinkle the oats mixture over the prepared layer. Bake at 375 degrees for 40 minutes or until light brown. Let stand for 10 minutes before serving.

Makes 8 (2/3-cup) servings

Nutrients Per Serving: Cal 203; Prot 2 g; Carbo 39 g; T Fat 5 g; (Saturated Fat 3 g); 23% Cal from Fat; Chol 12 mg; Fiber 4 g; Sod 46 mg; Calcium 12 mg

Cranberries grow best in bog areas—flat lands that can be flooded with water. If you visit Garrett County, Maryland's westernmost county, stop to see Cranesville Sub-Arctic Swamp, where you will find a rare pocket of sub-arctic vegetation and a cranberry bog. This land is thought to be the southernmost point of the glaciers that once covered much of North America. There are easy hiking trails and a boardwalk leading across the bog. For botanists this is a chance to see many rare species of plants. The bog area is owned and protected by the Nature Conservancy, which offers guided tours.

Blackberry Roly-Poly

2/3 cup baking mix
1/2 cup milk
3 tablespoons sugar
3 tablespoons butter or margarine, melted
1 pint fresh blackberries
3 tablespoons sugar
1 tablespoon cornstarch

Combine the baking mix, milk, 3 tablespoons sugar and butter in a bowl and mix well. Place the pastry on a lightly floured sheet of foil. Roll the pastry to fit a 5x9-inch loaf pan, allowing enough overhang to fold over.

Lift the foil and pastry together and fit into the baking pan. Spread the berries in the pastry-lined loaf pan. Sprinkle with a mixture of 3 tablespoons sugar and the cornstarch. Fold only the pastry over the berries, sealing the top and ends. Bake at 425 degrees for 25 minutes. Serve warm with cream, ice cream or lemon sauce.

Serves 4

Nutrients Per Serving: Cal 306; Prot 5 g; Carbo 51 g; T Fat 10 g; (Saturated Fat 6 g); 29% Cal from Fat; Chol 27 mg; Fiber 5 g; Sod 317 mg; Calcium 95 mg

It is worth your while to seek out these sweet little black beauties. A cup of blackberries has a respectable nine grams of dietary fiber, which is a sizeable portion of the recommended twenty-five to forty-five grams of fiber per day.

Chocolate Bread Pudding

1 1/2 cups bread cubes
2 cups fat-free milk
1/2 cup egg substitute
1/3 cup plus 1 tablespoon sugar
1/4 cup baking cocoa
1/2 cup walnuts, chopped

Arrange the bread cubes in a buttered shallow 2-quart baking dish. Whisk the fat-free milk, egg substitute, sugar and baking cocoa in a bowl until blended. Stir in the walnuts.

Pour the chocolate mixture over the bread cubes and stir. Place the baking dish in a larger baking pan. Add enough water to the baking pan to come halfway up the side of the baking dish. Bake at 350 degrees for 1 hour or until a knife inserted in the center comes out clean. Serve with milk, cream or ice cream.

Makes 6 (2/3-cup) servings

Nutrients Per Serving: Cal 182; Prot 8 g; Carbo 24 g; T Fat 7 g; (Saturated Fat 1 g); 33% Cal from Fat; Chol 2 mg; Fiber 1 g; Sod 118 mg; Calcium 126 mg

Tofu Pumpkin Pudding

10 ounces silken tofu
1 (28-ounce) can pumpkin
1/2 cup sugar
2 teaspoons cinnamon
1 teaspoon vanilla extract
1/8 teaspoon ground cloves

Process the tofu in a food processor until smooth. Add the pumpkin. Process until puréed. Add the sugar, cinnamon, vanilla and cloves. Process until blended. Spoon the tofu mixture into a 2-quart baking dish. Bake at 350 degrees for 30 minutes. Serve hot or cold.

Serves 8

Nutrients Per Serving: Cal 104; Prot 4 g; Carbo 21 g; T Fat 1 g; (Saturated Fat <1 g); 11% Cal from Fat; Chol 0 mg; Fiber 4 g; Sod 17 mg; Calcium 28 mg

Pecan Delights

Crust
1/2 cup (1 stick) butter, softened
3 ounces cream cheese, softened
1 cup flour
1 tablespoon sugar
1/8 teaspoon salt

Pecan Filling
2 tablespoons butter, melted
1 1/2 cups packed light brown sugar
2 eggs, lightly beaten
1 tablespoon vanilla extract
1 cup chopped pecans

For the crust, beat the butter and cream cheese in a mixing bowl until light and fluffy. Add the flour, sugar and salt. Beat until blended. Shape the cream cheese mixture into 24 small balls. Press each ball over the bottom and up the side of a miniature muffin cup.

For the filling, drizzle the butter over the brown sugar in a bowl. Add the eggs and vanilla and mix well. Stir in the pecans. Fill the prepared muffin cups 2/3 full. Bake at 350 degrees for 15 minutes. Reduce the oven temperature to 250 degrees. Bake for 15 minutes longer.

Makes 2 dozen

Nutrients Per Serving: Cal 169; Prot 2 g; Carbo 19 g; T Fat 10 g; (Saturated Fat 4 g); 52% Cal from Fat; Chol 35 mg; Fiber 1 g; Sod 82 mg; Calcium 22 mg

The pecan tree is a species of hickory that is native to the Mississippi River valley. The pecan nut was prized by the Native Americans and cultivated by Thomas Jefferson, who sent trees to Mount Vernon in Washington, D.C. There are more than three hundred varieties of pecans grown in the United States, mostly in the South and Southwest.

Chocolate Peanut Delight

1 (18-ounce) package chocolate sandwich cookies
6 tablespoons margarine, melted
1/2 gallon vanilla or chocolate chip ice cream, slightly softened
1 (12-ounce) jar fudge sauce
1 (12-ounce) package Spanish peanuts
8 ounces frozen whipped topping, thawed

Process the cookies in a food processor until crushed. Reserve 1/3 to 1/2 cup of the crumbs. Stir the margarine into the crumbs. Spread the crumb mixture over the bottom of a 9x13-inch dish sprayed with nonstick cooking spray.

Spread the ice cream over the prepared layer. Drizzle with the fudge sauce and sprinkle with the peanuts. Top with the whipped topping and sprinkle with the reserved cookie crumbs. Freeze, covered, until set. Sprinkle with chocolate chips and/or peanuts for variety.

Serves 15

Nutrients Per Serving: Cal 593; Prot 11 g; Carbo 61 g; T Fat 35 g; (Saturated Fat 12 g); 52% Cal from Fat; Chol 31 mg; Fiber 4 g; Sod 372 mg; Calcium 145 mg

This is a great summer dessert and SO tasty! The ingredients can be modified to produce a lower fat and lower calorie dessert . Use lite or fat-free ice cream, fat-free whipped topping, and reduce the amounts of fudge sauce and Spanish peanuts. The flavor will still be great.

Heavenly Dessert

4 egg whites
3/4 cup sugar
1/4 teaspoon cream of tartar
4 egg yolks
2 eggs
3/4 cup sugar
5 tablespoons lemon juice
1/8 teaspoon salt
2 cups whipping cream

Beat the egg whites in a mixing bowl until frothy. Add a mixture of 3/4 cup sugar and the cream of tartar gradually, beating constantly until stiff peaks form. Spread the egg white mixture in a greased 9x12-inch baking pan. Bake at 275 degrees for 1 hour. Let stand until cool.

Beat the egg yolks and eggs lightly in a mixing bowl. Stir in 3/4 cup sugar, the lemon juice and salt. Pour the mixture into a double boiler.

Cook for 8 to 10 minutes or until thickened, stirring frequently. Let stand until cool. Beat the whipping cream in a mixing bowl until soft peaks form. Fold 1/2 of the whipped cream into the lemon mixture. Spread the lemon mixture over the baked layer. Top with the remaining whipped cream. Chill, covered, for several hours before serving.

Serves 12

Nutrients Per Serving: Cal 273; Prot 4 g; Carbo 27 g; T Fat 17 g; (Saturated Fat 10 g); 56% Cal from Fat; Chol 161 mg; Fiber <1 g; Sod 71 mg; Calcium 39 mg

Here are a few tips to follow when beating egg whites: Eggs are easier to separate when cold, but beat to a greater volume at room temperature. For best results, separate eggs as soon as they are taken out of the refrigerator, then let them come to room temperature before beating. Cream of tartar increases volume and stabilizes the egg whites when baking. Egg whites that contain even a speck of yolk will not whip to maximum volume. And, finally, always use a clean bowl and clean beaters to beat egg whites.

Bonnie Butter Cake

2³/4 cups sifted flour
2¹/2 teaspoons baking powder
1 teaspoon salt
1³/4 cups sugar
2/3 cup butter or margarine, softened
2 eggs
1¹/2 teaspoons vanilla extract
1¹/4 cups whole or fat-free milk

Sift the flour, baking powder and salt together. Combine the sugar, butter, eggs and vanilla in a mixing bowl. Beat at high speed for 5 minutes or until light and fluffy. Add the flour mixture alternately with the milk, beating constantly at low speed until blended.

Spoon the batter into 2 greased and floured 9-inch cake pans or a 9x13-inch cake pan. Bake at 350 degrees for 25 to 30 minutes for the 9-inch cake pans or 45 minutes for the 9x13-inch cake pan. Cool in pan on a wire rack. Serve plain or spread with your favorite frosting.

Serves 12

Nutrients Per Serving: Cal 328; Prot 5 g; Carbo 51 g; T Fat 12 g; (Saturated Fat 7 g); 33% Cal from Fat; Chol 67 mg; Fiber 1 g; Sod 423 mg; Calcium 98 mg

Sour Cream Pound Cake

3 cups cake flour
1/4 teaspoon baking soda
3 cups sugar
1 cup (2 sticks) butter, softened
6 egg yolks
1 cup sour cream
6 egg whites

Sift the cake flour and baking soda together. Beat the sugar and butter in a mixing bowl until creamy, scraping the bowl occasionally. Add the egg yolks 1 at a time, beating well after each addition. Add the flour mixture to the creamed mixture alternately with the sour cream, beating well after each addition.

Beat the egg whites in a mixing bowl until stiff peaks form. Fold the egg whites into the batter. Spoon the batter into a buttered and floured 12-cup bundt pan. Bake at 300 degrees for 1 1/2 hours or until a wooden pick inserted in the center comes out clean. Cool in pan for 15 minutes. Invert onto a wire rack to cool completely.

Serves 16

Nutrients Per Serving: Cal 399; Prot 5 g; Carbo 58 g; T Fat 17 g; (Saturated Fat 10 g); 37% Cal from Fat; Chol 117 mg; Fiber <1 g; Sod 169 mg; Calcium 33 mg

Buttermilk Coffee Cake

Indulge in some delectable treats without overdoing by following these simple tips:
* Check your fuel gauge. Listen to your stomach when it tells you it is full.
* Eat sensually. Get out the pretty plate and really enjoy the dessert or other food items.
* Don't starve yourself. Starving typically leads to overeating, especially of more high calorie foods.

3 cups sifted flour
2 cups sugar
1 teaspoon cinnamon
1 teaspoon salt
1/2 teaspoon nutmeg
1 cup (2 sticks) margarine or butter
1 cup buttermilk
2 eggs, beaten
1 teaspoon baking soda

Sift the flour, sugar, cinnamon, salt and nutmeg into a bowl and mix well. Cut in the margarine until crumbly. Reserve 1 1/2 cups of the crumb mixture. Whisk the buttermilk and eggs in a bowl.

Add the buttermilk mixture and baking soda to the remaining crumb mixture and stir just until moistened. Spoon the batter into 2 greased and floured 8-inch cake pans. Sprinkle with the reserved crumb mixture. Bake at 400 degrees for 30 minutes. Cool in pans for 10 minutes. Invert onto a wire rack to cool completely.

Serves 16

Nutrients Per Serving: Cal 292; Prot 4 g; Carbo 42 g; T Fat 12 g; (Saturated Fat 3 g); 38% Cal from Fat; Chol 27 mg; Fiber 1 g; Sod 382 mg; Calcium 29 mg

State Fair Coffee Cake

2 cups flour
1 teaspoon baking powder
1 cup (2 sticks) butter or margarine, softened
1 cup sugar
2 eggs, or equivalent amount of egg substitute
1 cup sour cream or low-fat sour cream
1/2 teaspoon vanilla extract
1/2 teaspoon almond extract
1/2 cup sugar
1 tablespoon baking cocoa
1 teaspoon cinnamon
1/2 cup chopped walnuts

Mix the flour and baking powder together. Beat the butter and 1 cup sugar in a mixing bowl until creamy, scraping the bowl occasionally. Add the eggs and beat until blended. Beat in the sour cream and flavorings. Add the flour mixture and beat until smooth.

Combine 1/2 cup sugar, baking cocoa and cinnamon in a bowl and mix well. Stir in the walnuts. Spoon 1/3 of the batter into a greased and floured 10-inch tube or bundt pan. Sprinkle with 3/4 of the walnut mixture. Spread with the remaining batter and sprinkle with the remaining walnut mixture. Bake at 350 degrees for 1 hour. Cool in pan for 10 minutes. Invert onto a wire rack to cool completely.

Serves 16

Nutrients Per Serving: Cal 297; Prot 4 g; Carbo 32 g; T Fat 18 g; (Saturated Fat 9 g); 53% Cal from Fat; Chol 64 mg; Fiber 1 g; Sod 164 mg; Calcium 46 mg

Old-Fashioned Carrot Cake

2¹/4 cups flour
2 teaspoons each salt, baking soda and cinnamon
2 cups sugar
1¹/4 cups vegetable oil
4 eggs
3 cups coarsely grated carrots
1 cup chopped walnuts or pecans
Cream Cheese Frosting (below) (optional)

Sift the flour, salt, baking soda and cinnamon together. Combine the sugar, oil and eggs in a mixing bowl. Beat at medium speed for 2 minutes. Add the flour mixture. Beat at low speed for 1 minute. Stir in the carrots and walnuts. Spoon the batter into a greased and floured 9x13-inch cake pan. Bake at 300 degrees for 1 hour or until the cake tests done. Cool in pan on a wire rack. Serve plain or spread with Cream Cheese Frosting and sprinkle with additional chopped walnuts or pecans.

Serves 15

Nutrients Per Serving: Cal 414; Prot 5 g; Carbo 44 g; T Fat 25 g; (Saturated Fat 3 g); 53% Cal from Fat; Chol 57 mg; Fiber 2 g; Sod 503 mg; Calcium 24 mg
Nutritional profile does not include Cream Cheese Frosting.

A delicious and hearty cake that receives rave reviews even without the frosting.

Cream Cheese Frosting

8 ounces cream cheese, softened
¹/4 cup (¹/2 stick) margarine, softened
2 teaspoons vanilla extract
1 (1-pound) package confectioners' sugar

Beat the cream cheese and margarine in a mixing bowl until creamy. Add the vanilla and beat until blended. Add the confectioners' sugar gradually, beating constantly until of a spreading consistency. You may add a small amount of milk to attain a spreading consistency.

Serves 15

Nutrients Per Serving: Cal 197; Prot 1 g; Carbo 31 g; T Fat 8 g; (Saturated Fat 4 g); 37% Cal from Fat; Chol 17 mg; Fiber 0 g; Sod 81 mg; Calcium 14 mg

Lady Baltimore Cake

Cake
3 cups sifted cake flour
1 tablespoon baking powder
1/2 teaspoon salt
1/2 cup milk
1/2 cup water
3/4 cup shortening
2 cups sugar
1 teaspoon vanilla extract
6 egg whites, at room
   temperature

Filling and Assembly
11/2 cups sugar
1/8 teaspoon cream of tartar
6 tablespoons water
2 egg whites
1 teaspoon vanilla extract
1/2 teaspoon lemon extract
11/2 cups chopped pecans
1 cup chopped raisins
1 cup chopped dried figs
Seven-Minute Frosting
   (page 150)
Walnut halves (optional)

Was this cake named for the first lady of our state or the city of Baltimore? There are conflicting reports, but either way this is a very distinctive cake. Three layers high with a rich filling makes it appropriate for those special occasions.

For the cake, mix the cake flour, baking powder and salt together. Combine the milk and water in a measuring cup and mix well. Beat the shortening in a mixing bowl until creamy. Add the sugar gradually, beating constantly until blended. Add the flour mixture alternately with the milk mixture, beginning and ending with the flour mixture and beating well after each addition. Beat in the vanilla. Beat the egg whites in a mixing bowl until stiff peaks form. Fold the egg whites into the batter. Spoon the batter into 3 greased and floured 9-inch cake pans. Bake at 350 degrees for 25 minutes or until the layers test done. Cool in pans for 10 minutes. Remove to a wire rack to cool completely.

For the filling, combine the sugar and cream of tartar in a saucepan and mix well. Stir in the water. Cook over medium heat until the mixture comes to a boil and the sugar dissolves, stirring frequently. Continue cooking until the mixture registers 240 degrees on a candy thermometer, soft-ball stage, stirring frequently. Beat the egg whites in a mixing bowl at medium speed until foamy, adding the hot sugar syrup gradually. Beat at high speed until stiff peaks form. Beat in the flavorings. Stir in the pecans, raisins and figs.

To assemble, reserve 1/4 cup of the filling. Spread the remaining filling between the layers. Spread the frosting over the top and side of the cake. Garnish with the reserved filling and walnut halves.

Serves 16

Nutrients Per Serving: Cal 543; Prot 6 g; Carbo 93 g; T Fat 18 g; (Saturated Fat 3 g);
29% Cal from Fat; Chol 1 mg; Fiber 4 g; Sod 223 mg; Calcium 10 mg
Nutritional profile includes the frosting.

Seven-Minute Frosting

1 cup sugar
1 egg white, at room temperature
1 tablespoon light corn syrup
1/8 teaspoon salt
3 tablespoons cold water
1 teaspoon vanilla

Combine the sugar, egg white, corn syrup and salt in the top of a double boiler. Add the cold water. Beat at low speed for 30 seconds or just until blended.

Place over boiling water. Beat at high speed for 7 minutes or until stiff peaks form. Remove from heat. Place the double boiler top over a bowl of cold water. Let stand for 5 minutes. Stir in the vanilla.

Serves 16

Nutrients Per Serving: Cal 53; Prot <1 g; Carbo 13 g; T Fat 0 g; (Saturated Fat 0 g); 0% Cal from Fat; Chol 0 mg; Fiber 0 g; Sod 23 mg; Calcium <1 mg

Triple Chocolate Cake

1 (2-layer) package chocolate cake mix
1 (4-ounce) package chocolate instant pudding mix
1 1/4 cups water
1 cup (6 ounces) chocolate chips
1/4 cup vegetable oil
4 eggs, lightly beaten

Combine the cake mix, pudding mix, water, chocolate chips, oil and eggs in a bowl. Stir with a fork for 2 minutes or until mixed. Spoon the batter into a 9x13-inch cake pan sprayed with nonstick cooking spray.

Bake at 350 degrees for 40 to 45 minutes or until the top springs back when lightly touched. Cool in pan on a wire rack. Cut into squares to serve.

Serves 15

Nutrients Per Serving: Cal 283; Prot 4 g; Carbo 39 g; T Fat 14 g; (Saturated Fat 4 g); 42% Cal from Fat; Chol 57 mg; Fiber 2 g; Sod 401 mg; Calcium 64 mg

Turtle Cake

1 (2-layer) package German chocolate cake mix
1 (14-ounce) package caramels
1/2 cup evaporated milk
1/2 cup (1 stick) margarine
1 cup (6 ounces) chocolate chips
1 cup chopped pecans

Prepare the cake mix using package directions. Spoon 1/2 of the batter into a 9x13-inch cake pan sprayed with nonstick cooking spray. Bake at 350 degrees for 15 minutes.

Combine the caramels, evaporated milk and margarine in a saucepan. Heat over medium heat until blended, stirring frequently. Drizzle the caramel mixture over the hot baked layer. Sprinkle with the chocolate chips and pecans.

Spread the remaining batter over the top. Bake at 350 degrees for 20 minutes. Cool in pan on a wire rack. Serve with whipped cream.

Makes 24 (2-inch) squares

Nutrients Per Serving: Cal 302; Prot 4 g; Carbo 36 g; T Fat 17 g; (Saturated Fat 5 g); 49% Cal from Fat; Chol 29 mg; Fiber 2 g; Sod 236 mg; Calcium 47 mg

Smith Island Cake

Cake
1 cup flour
1 teaspoon baking powder
2 cups sugar
1 cup (2 sticks) butter, softened
5 eggs, beaten
1 tablespoon vanilla extract
1/2 cup evaporated milk
1/2 cup water
1 3/4 cups flour

Chocolate Icing
1/2 cup (1 stick) butter
6 tablespoons baking cocoa
1 (1-pound) package
    confectioners' sugar
3/4 cup cream
2 teaspoons vanilla extract
1/8 teaspoon salt

For the cake, mix 1 cup flour and baking powder together. Beat the sugar and butter in a mixing bowl until creamy, scraping the bowl occasionally. Add the beaten eggs and beat until blended. Beat in the vanilla.

Mix the evaporated milk and water in a bowl. Add the evaporated milk mixture alternately with 1 3/4 cups flour and the flour mixture, adding the flour mixture last and beating well after each addition. Spoon the batter into 5 to 7 greased and floured 8-inch cake pans. Bake at 350 degrees for 7 minutes. Cool in pans for 10 minutes. Remove to a wire rack to cool completely.

For the icing, heat the butter in a saucepan. Stir in the baking cocoa. Add the confectioners' sugar, cream, vanilla and salt and mix well. Cook for 10 minutes, stirring frequently. Remove from the heat and beat with an electric mixer if the icing becomes lumpy. Spread the hot icing between the layers and over the top and side of the cake. Let stand until set.

Serves 12

Nutrients Per Serving: Cal 692; Prot 7 g; Carbo 96 g; T Fat 32 g; (Saturated Fat 19 g); 41% Cal from Fat; Chol 174 mg; Fiber 1 g; Sod 343 mg; Calcium 81 mg

Smith Island is Maryland's only inhabited offshore island in the Chesapeake Bay. The island has three small towns and fewer than five hundred inhabitants. The original English and Welsh settlers arrived in 1659 and became farmers. Today's residents primarily make their living by harvesting crabs and oysters in the Bay.

Pumpkin Chocolate Chip Muffins

4 cups all-purpose flour
2 2/3 cups whole wheat flour
4 cups sugar
2 tablespoons cinnamon
4 teaspoons baking soda
1 teaspoon baking powder
1 teaspoon ground cloves
1 teaspoon nutmeg
1 teaspoon salt
8 eggs, lightly beaten

4 cups puréed baked fresh
    pumpkin
3/4 cup unsweetened
    applesauce
1/2 cup (1 stick) margarine,
    melted
4 cups (24 ounces) chocolate
    chips
2 cups chopped walnuts

Combine the all-purpose flour, whole wheat flour, sugar, cinnamon, baking soda, baking powder, cloves, nutmeg and salt in a bowl and mix well. Mix the eggs, pumpkin, applesauce and margarine in a bowl. Stir the chocolate chips and walnuts into the pumpkin mixture.

Pour the pumpkin mixture over the flour mixture and fold with a rubber spatula just until the ingredients are moistened. Fill paper-lined muffin cups 2/3 full. Bake at 350 degrees for 15 to 20 minutes or until the muffins spring back when touched lightly.

Makes 5 dozen muffins

Nutrients Per Serving: Cal 213; Prot 4 g; Carbo 33 g; T Fat 9 g; (Saturated Fat 3 g); 34% Cal from Fat; Chol 28 mg; Fiber 2 g; Sod 159 mg; Calcium 25 mg

Recapture that just-baked taste in day-old muffins. Wet a microwave-safe white paper towel and squeeze to remove the excess moisture. Wrap the dampened paper towel around one or two muffins. Microwave on High for about forty seconds for one muffin or one minute for two muffins.

Chocolate Fudge

2/3 cup evaporated milk
1¹/2 cups sugar
2 tablespoons butter or margarine
¹/4 teaspoon salt
2 cups miniature marshmallows
1¹/2 cups (9 ounces) semisweet chocolate chips
¹/2 cup chopped pecans or walnuts
1 teaspoon vanilla extract

Combine the evaporated milk, sugar, butter and salt in a saucepan. Bring to a boil over medium heat, stirring constantly. Remove from heat. Stir in the marshmallows, chocolate chips, pecans and vanilla.

Stir for 1 minute or until the marshmallows melt. Spread the chocolate mixture in a buttered 8x8-inch dish. Let stand until set. Cut into squares.

Makes 16 (2-ounce) servings

Nutrients Per Serving: Cal 226; Prot 2 g; Carbo 36 g; T Fat 10 g; (Saturated Fat 5 g); 37% Cal from Fat; Chol 7 mg; Fiber 1 g; Sod 66 mg; Calcium 36 mg

This recipe is simple to make and quite popular with our testers. Be sure to premeasure the marshmallows, chocolate chips, vanilla, and chopped pecans.

Grasshopper Brownies

Brownies
1 (21-ounce) package
    brownie mix
$1/2$ cup water
$1/2$ cup vegetable oil
1 egg

Cream Cheese Filling
$1/2$ cup (1 stick) margarine,
    softened
3 ounces cream cheese,
    softened
$2^1/2$ cups confectioners' sugar
Mint extract to taste
Green food coloring

Chocolate Glaze
1 cup (6 ounces) semisweet
    chocolate chips
$1/3$ cup margarine

For the brownies, grease the bottom of a 9x13-inch baking pan. Combine the brownie mix, water, oil and egg in a bowl. Beat 50 strokes with a spoon or until well mixed. Spread the batter in the prepared pan. Bake at 350 degrees for 30 to 35 minutes or until the edges pull from the sides of the pan. Let stand until cool.

For the filling, beat the margarine and cream cheese in a mixing bowl until light and fluffy. Add the confectioners' sugar, flavoring and several drops of food coloring. Beat until smooth. Spread the cream cheese filling over the baked layer.

For the glaze, combine the chocolate chips and margarine in a saucepan. Cook over low heat until blended, stirring constantly. Cool for 15 minutes. Drizzle the glaze over the prepared layers. Chill, covered, for 1 hour before cutting into bars.

Makes 4 dozen bars

Nutrients Per Serving: Cal 154; Prot 1 g; Carbo 18 g; T Fat 9 g; (Saturated Fat 2 g); 52% Cal from Fat; Chol 6 mg; Fiber 1 g; Sod 82 mg; Calcium 7 mg

Raspberry Coconut Bars

1²/3 cups graham cracker crumbs
1/2 cup (1 stick) butter or margarine, melted
1 (7-ounce) package flaked coconut
1 (14-ounce) can sweetened condensed milk
1 cup red raspberry jam
1/3 cup chopped walnuts
1/2 cup (3 ounces) semisweet chocolate chips, melted
1/4 cup chopped white baking chocolate, melted

Combine the cracker crumbs and butter in a bowl and mix well. Pat the crumb mixture over the bottom of a 9x13-inch baking pan. Sprinkle with the coconut and drizzle with the condensed milk. Bake at 350 degrees for 20 to 25 minutes or until light brown. Let stand until cool.

Spread the jam over the baked layer. Chill, covered, for 3 to 4 hours. Sprinkle with the walnuts. Drizzle the semisweet chocolate and white chocolate in a decorative pattern over the top. Chill, covered, until set. Cut into bars.

Makes 2 dozen (1¹/2x3-inch) bars

Nutrients Per Serving: Cal 227; Prot 3 g; Carbo 30 g; T Fat 11 g; (Saturated Fat 7 g); 44% Cal from Fat; Chol 17 mg; Fiber 1 g; Sod 123 mg; Calcium 59 mg

Anise Cookies

1 envelope dry yeast
1/2 cup lukewarm water
1 cup flour
1 teaspoon salt
1 cup (2 sticks) butter, softened
1 cup shortening, at room temperature
3 tablespoons sugar
4 teaspoons anise extract
4 cups flour
1 teaspoon baking powder
Red and green tinted sugar to taste

Dissolve the yeast in the lukewarm water in a large bowl and stir. Add 1 cup flour and salt and mix well. Stir in the butter, shortening, sugar and flavoring. Add a mixture of 4 cups flour and baking powder and mix well.

Divide the dough into 6 to 8 equal portions. Shape each portion into a ball and then into a long thin log; slice. Arrange the slices cut side up on a cookie sheet. Bake at 350 degrees for 25 minutes or until golden brown. Coat the warm cookies with the tinted sugar. Cool on a wire rack.

Makes 10 dozen cookies

Nutrients Per Cookie: Cal 49; Prot 1 g; Carbo 4 g; T Fat 3 g; (Saturated Fat 1 g);
60% Cal from Fat; Chol 4 mg; Fiber <1 g; Sod 39 mg; Calcium 4 mg

Anise was used as a condiment by the Greeks, Romans, and Hebrews. It is similar in taste to licorice and is most often used in desserts and liqueurs. Mexico is the largest producer of anise.

Prize-Winning Chocolate Chip Cookies

1 cup (2 sticks) butter, softened
1/2 cup peanut butter
1 cup packed brown sugar
1/2 cup sugar
2 eggs, beaten
2 cups flour
1 teaspoon baking soda
11/2 cups rolled oats
1/2 cup chopped walnuts
1/2 cup raisins
1 cup (6 ounces) chocolate chips
1/2 cup flaked coconut

Grease a 14-inch baking pan. Beat the butter and peanut butter in a mixing bowl until creamy. Add the brown sugar and sugar and stir until smooth. Add the eggs and mix gently.

Sift the flour and baking soda together. Add the flour mixture 1/2 at a time to the creamed mixture, mixing well after each addition. Stir in the oats. Add the walnuts, raisins and chocolate chips and mix well.

Pat the dough over the bottom of the prepared pan. Bake at 375 degrees for 10 minutes. Sprinkle with the coconut and pat lightly with the back of a spoon. Bake for 15 minutes longer or until golden brown.

To serve, slice with a pizza cutter into quarters and then slice each quarter into sixths. For individual cookies, stir the coconut into the cookie dough and drop by heaping teaspoonfuls onto a greased cookie sheet. Bake for 10 minutes or until golden brown. Makes 5 dozen drop cookies.

Makes 2 dozen pan cookies

Nutrients Per Pan Cookie: Cal 288; Prot 5 g; Carbo 35 g; T Fat 16 g; (Saturated Fat 8 g); 47% Cal from Fat; Chol 38 mg; Fiber 2 g; Sod 170 mg; Calcium 22 mg

Forgotten Cookies

2 egg whites
1/4 teaspoon cream of tartar
1/8 teaspoon salt
2/3 cup sugar

1 teaspoon vanilla extract
1 cup (6 ounces) miniature
    chocolate chips

Beat the egg whites, cream of tartar and salt in a mixing bowl until soft peaks form. Add the sugar gradually, beating constantly at high speed. Add the vanilla and continue beating until stiff glossy peaks form. Fold in the chocolate chips. Drop by teaspoonfuls onto a cookie sheet lined with foil. Place in a preheated 350-degree oven. Turn off the oven. Let stand in the oven with the door closed for 8 to 10 hours.

Makes 2 dozen cookies

Nutrients Per Cookie: Cal 58; Prot 1 g; Carbo 10 g; T Fat 2 g; (Saturated Fat 1 g);
31% Cal from Fat; Chol 0 mg; Fiber <1 g; Sod 18 mg; Calcium 3 mg

Delicious Cookies

3 1/2 cups flour
1 teaspoon salt
1 teaspoon baking soda
1 teaspoon cream of tartar
1 cup sugar
1 cup packed brown sugar
1 cup (2 sticks) butter, softened

1 cup vegetable oil
1 egg
1 teaspoon vanilla extract
1 cup crisp rice cereal
1 cup rolled oats
1 cup shredded coconut
1/2 chopped pecans

Mix the flour, salt, baking soda and cream of tartar in a bowl. Beat the sugar, brown sugar, butter, oil, egg and vanilla in a mixing bowl until creamy. Add the flour mixture and beat until blended. Stir in the cereal, oats, coconut and pecans. Shape the dough into 1-inch balls. Arrange the balls 2 inches apart on cookie sheets; flatten with a fork. Bake at 350 degrees for 8 to 15 minutes or until light brown. Cool on cookie sheets for 2 minutes. Remove to wire racks to cool completely. The dough may be frozen and baked at a later date.

Makes 6 dozen cookies

Nutrients Per Cookie: Cal 114; Prot 1 g; Carbo 12 g; T Fat 7 g; (Saturated Fat 2 g);
53% Cal from Fat; Chol 10 mg; Fiber <1 g; Sod 85 mg; Calcium 5 mg

Very low in fat, these meringue cookies are a terrific addition to a cookie platter. For variety, add a drop or two of food coloring . . . green for Christmas and red for a lite Valentine's Day treat.

Polish Cookies (Mazurki)

1$1/2$ cups sugar
1 cup (2 sticks) butter or margarine, softened
6 eggs, beaten
2 cups flour
2 teaspoons baking powder
$1/2$ teaspoon vanilla extract
$1/2$ teaspoon almond extract
1$1/2$ cups chopped walnuts
$1/2$ cup raisins
$1/3$ to $1/2$ cup confectioners' sugar

Beat the sugar and butter in a mixing bowl until creamy. Add the beaten eggs and mix until blended. Add the flour $1/2$ cup at a time, beating well after each addition. Add the baking powder and flavorings and mix well. Stir in the walnuts and raisins.

Pat the dough over the bottom of a 10x15-inch baking pan sprayed lightly with nonstick cooking spray. Sprinkle with the confectioners' sugar. Bake at 350 degrees for 20 to 25 minutes or until light brown. Cool in pan on a wire rack. Cut into triangles.

Makes 4 dozen cookies

Nutrients Per Cookie: Cal 120; Prot 2 g; Carbo 13 g; T Fat 7 g; (Saturated Fat 3 g); 51% Cal from Fat; Chol 37 mg; Fiber <1 g; Sod 68 mg; Calcium 21 mg

What exactly is a flavor extract? This recipe uses both a vanilla extract and an almond extract. Extracts are concentrated flavorings that come from different foods and plants. Anise, vanilla, peppermint, and almond extracts are made by distilling fruits, seeds, or leaves. The extract, versus the imitation flavoring, is more concentrated, so "a little goes a long way."

Swedish Rose Hips

1/2 cup (1 stick) butter, softened
1/2 cup (1 stick) margarine, softened
1/2 cup sugar
2 cups flour
1/2 to 3/4 cup favorite jam or jelly

Beat the butter, margarine and sugar in a mixing bowl until creamy. Add the flour and beat until blended. Shape the dough into 1-inch balls.

Arrange the balls on ungreased cookie sheets. Make an indentation in the top of each ball. Fill the indentations with the jam. Bake at 350 degrees for 12 to 15 minutes or until light brown. Cool on cookie sheets for 2 minutes. Remove to wire racks to cool completely.

Makes 4 dozen cookies

Nutrients Per Cookie: Cal 75; Prot 1 g; Carbo 10 g; T Fat 4 g; (Saturated Fat 2 g); 46% Cal from Fat; Chol 5 mg; Fiber <1 g; Sod 43 mg; Calcium 3 mg

Lite Pumpkin Pie

1 (30-ounce) can pumpkin pie filling
16 ounces frozen lite whipped topping, thawed
1/2 teaspoon ginger
1/2 teaspoon cinnamon
1 (9-inch) graham cracker pie shell

Combine the pie filling, whipped topping, ginger and cinnamon in a bowl and mix well. Spoon the pumpkin filling into the pie shell. Freeze, covered, for 4 hours or until firm.

Serves 8

Nutrients Per Serving: Cal 384; Prot 2 g; Carbo 60 g; T Fat 14 g; (Saturated Fat 8 g); 33% Cal from Fat; Chol 0 mg; Fiber 9 g; Sod 392 mg; Calcium 46 mg

Butterscotch Pumpkin Pie

1 cup fat-free milk
1 (4-serving) package butterscotch sugar-free instant pudding mix
1 cup canned pumpkin
1/2 teaspoon nutmeg
1/2 teaspoon cinnamon
1 (9-inch) graham cracker pie shell
1 cup frozen lite whipped topping, thawed
1 teaspoon vanilla extract

Combine the fat-free milk and pudding mix in a bowl and beat until blended. Stir in the pumpkin, nutmeg and cinnamon. Spoon the pumpkin mixture into the pie shell. Chill, covered, for 2 hours or longer.

Combine the whipped topping and vanilla in a bowl and mix well. Top each serving with a dollop of the whipped topping mixture.

Serves 8

Nutrients Per Serving: Cal 199; Prot 3 g; Carbo 28 g; T Fat 9 g; (Saturated Fat 3 g); 39% Cal from Fat; Chol 1 mg; Fiber 2 g; Sod 334 mg; Calcium 49 mg

Swedish Apple Pie

Pie
4 cups cooked sliced apples
1/2 cup sugar
2 tablespoons flour
1/8 teaspoon salt
1 egg
1 teaspoon vanilla extract
1 cup sour cream
1 unbaked (9-inch) pie shell

Topping
1/2 cup sugar
1/2 cup flour
1 teaspoon cinnamon
1/2 cup (1 stick) margarine,
    softened

For the pie, mash the apples lightly in a bowl. Stir in the sugar, flour and salt. Whisk the egg and vanilla in a bowl. Add the egg mixture to the apple mixture and mix well. Fold in the sour cream. Spoon the apple mixture into the pie shell. Bake at 350 degrees for 40 to 50 minutes.

For the topping, mix the sugar, flour and cinnamon in a bowl. Add the margarine and mix until crumbly. Sprinkle the crumb mixture over the hot filling. Bake for 15 minutes longer.

Serves 8

Nutrients Per Serving: Cal 464; Prot 4 g; Carbo 56 g; T Fat 26 g; (Saturated Fat 8 g); 49% Cal from Fat; Chol 39 mg; Fiber 3 g; Sod 311 mg; Calcium 49 mg

Strawberry Gelatin Pie

Crust

1 cup baking mix
1/4 cup (1/2 stick) butter, softened
2 tablespoons boiling water

Strawberry Filling

3/4 cup sugar
3 tablespoons cornstarch
1 1/2 cups water
1 (3-ounce) package strawberry gelatin
1/8 teaspoon salt
1 pint fresh strawberries
Frozen whipped topping, thawed (optional)

For the crust, combine the baking mix and butter in a bowl and mix until crumbly. Add the boiling water and stir until a dough forms. Press the dough over the bottom and up the side of a 9-inch pie plate. Bake at 375 degrees for 8 to 10 minutes or until light brown. Let stand until cool.

For the filling, combine the sugar and cornstarch in a saucepan and mix well. Stir in the water. Cook until thickened, stirring frequently. Stir in the gelatin and salt. Cook until the gelatin dissolves, stirring constantly. Cool slightly.

Slice the strawberries if desired. Add the strawberries to the gelatin mixture and mix gently. Spoon the strawberry mixture into the pastry-lined pie plate. Chill, covered, for several hours. Serve with whipped topping.

Serves 8

Nutrients Per Serving: Cal 254; Prot 4 g; Carbo 48 g; T Fat 6 g; (Saturated Fat 4 g); 21% Cal from Fat; Chol 16 mg; Fiber 2 g; Sod 280 mg; Calcium 32 mg

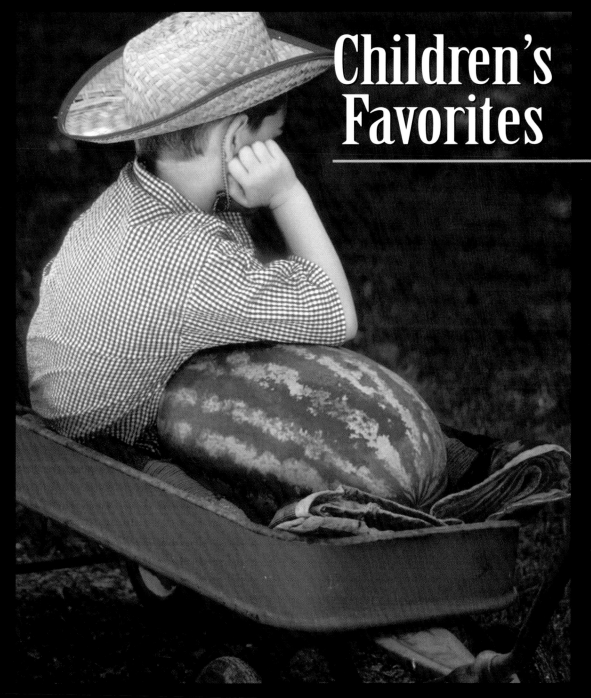

Children's Favorites

Children's Favorites

Muddy Buddies

1 cup (6 ounces) chocolate chips
1/2 cup peanut butter
1/4 cup (1/2 stick) margarine
1/4 teaspoon vanilla extract
12 cups Chex cereal
2 cups confectioners' sugar

Combine the chocolate chips, peanut butter and margarine in a large microwave-safe bowl. Microwave until blended; stir. Add the vanilla and mix well. Add the cereal and toss to coat. Let stand until cool.

Place the confectioners' sugar in a 2-gallon sealable plastic bag. Add the cereal mixture and seal tightly. Toss gently to coat.

Serves 24

Nutrients Per Serving: Cal 180; Prot 3 g; Carbo 29 g; T Fat 7 g; (Saturated Fat 2 g); 34% Cal from Fat; Chol 0 mg; Fiber 1 g; Sod 192 mg; Calcium 55 mg

Puppy Chow

2²/3 cups (16 ounces) chocolate chips
1/4 cup peanut butter
6 cups Crispix
1 cup confectioners' sugar

Place the chocolate chips in a microwave-safe bowl. Microwave on High for 1 minute; stir. Microwave for 30 seconds longer or until melted. Stir in the peanut butter. Add the cereal and stir until coated.

Place the confectioners' sugar in a 2-gallon sealable plastic bag. Add the cereal mixture and seal tightly. Shake gently until coated. Store in an airtight container in the refrigerator.

Serves 12

Nutrients Per Serving: Cal 319; Prot 4 g; Carbo 49 g; T Fat 15 g; (Saturated Fat 8 g); 39% Cal from Fat; Chol 0 mg; Fiber 3 g; Sod 150 mg; Calcium 17 mg

Snacks are important for children. They have high energy needs and small stomachs and are not always able to eat enough food in three meals to meet all of their nutrient needs. However, children should be taught to eat healthy snacks in reasonable portions.

Fruit Smoothies

1 cup plain low-fat yogurt
1 cup apple or orange juice
1 cup fresh or frozen unsweetened strawberries
1 banana, sliced

Combine the yogurt, apple juice, strawberries and banana in a blender or food processor. Process until smooth. Serve immediately.

Serves 2

Nutrients Per Serving: Cal 211; Prot 8 g; Carbo 42 g; T Fat 3 g; (Saturated Fat 1 g); 11% Cal from Fat; Chol 7 mg; Fiber 3 g; Sod 91 mg; Calcium 246 mg

Snack-in-a-Glass

1 cup fruit-flavor yogurt of choice
1 cup milk
1 cup fresh or frozen unsweetened blueberries, strawberries or peaches
2 teaspoons sugar
1/4 teaspoon vanilla or almond extract
2 or 3 ice cubes

Combine the yogurt, milk, blueberries, sugar and flavoring in a blender. Process on high until bubbly. Add the ice cubes 1 at a time, processing constantly until smooth. Pour into 4 glasses. Garnish with additional fruit. Serve immediately. Decrease the fat grams by using nonfat yogurt and 1% milk.

Serves 4

Nutrients Per Serving: Cal 129; Prot 5 g; Carbo 21 g; T Fat 4 g; (Saturated Fat 1 g); 24% Cal from Fat; Chol 8 mg; Fiber 1 g; Sod 67 mg; Calcium 75 mg

Smoothies are a simple way to add fruit and dairy products to a child's diet. They resemble milk shake-type drinks and are naturally sweet. Leftovers may be stored in the refrigerator for one day, or frozen as a "smoothie pop."

Stars and Spinach Soup

6 cups chicken broth
1 (10-ounce) package frozen chopped spinach
3/4 cup star-shape pasta
1 egg, beaten
1/4 cup grated Parmesan or Romano cheese
1/8 teaspoon pepper

Bring the broth to a boil in a saucepan. Microwave the spinach in a microwave-safe dish for 3 to 4 minutes. Drain the spinach in a colander, pressing to release any excess moisture.

Add the pasta to the boiling broth. Simmer for 5 to 10 minutes or until the pasta is tender. Stir in the spinach. Drizzle the egg into the broth mixture, stirring constantly. Add the cheese and pepper and mix well. Simmer just until heated through, stirring frequently. Ladle into soup bowls.

Serves 6

Nutrients Per Serving: Cal 128; Prot 11 g; Carbo 13 g; T Fat 4 g; (Saturated Fat 1 g); 26% Cal from Fat; Chol 38 mg; Fiber 2 g; Sod 884 mg; Calcium 115 mg

Walking Salad

1 apple
2 tablespoons peanut butter
10 raisins
10 peanuts, cashews or walnuts
1/4 cup granola cereal

Slice off the top of the apple and reserve. Remove the inside of the apple carefully, leaving a shell. Discard the core, reserving the apple pulp. Chop the reserved apple pulp into a bowl. Add the peanut butter, raisins, peanuts and granola to the chopped apple and mix well. Fill the apple shell with the peanut butter mixture; replace the top. Enjoy on your hike.

Serves 1

Nutrients Per Serving: Cal 444; Prot 13 g; Carbo 50 g; T Fat 25 g; (Saturated Fat 4 g); 47% Cal from Fat; Chol 0 mg; Fiber 8 g; Sod 207 mg; Calcium 40 mg

These apples are great to take on hikes and can be filled with other fruit, nut, or cereal combinations. Maryland offers a variety of scenic parks for families to hike and enjoy nature. Check out state parks at www.dnr.state.md.us/mdmap.html.

Fruit Salad Gelatin Mold

1 (15-ounce) can fruit cocktail
1 (3-ounce) package orange gelatin
8 ounces cream cheese, softened
1 cup heavy cream
3/4 cup chopped pecans

Drain the fruit cocktail, reserving the juice. Bring the reserved juice to a boil in a saucepan. Add the gelatin, stirring until dissolved. Let stand until cool. Chill until partially set.

Beat the cream cheese and heavy cream in a mixing bowl until blended. Add the gelatin mixture and pecans to the cream cheese mixture and mix well. Spoon the gelatin mixture into a mold. Chill, covered, until set. Invert onto a lettuce-lined serving platter.

Serves 8

Nutrients Per Serving: Cal 356; Prot 5 g; Carbo 22 g; T Fat 29 g; (Saturated Fat 14 g); 70% Cal from Fat; Chol 72 mg; Fiber 2 g; Sod 123 mg; Calcium 53 mg

Pretzel Salad

2 cups (4 ounces) crushed pretzels
1/2 cup (1 stick) margarine, melted
3 tablespoons sugar
8 ounces cream cheese, softened
8 ounces frozen whipped topping, thawed
1/2 cup sugar
1 (6-ounce) package strawberry gelatin
2 cups boiling water
1 (16-ounce) package frozen sliced sweetened strawberries
1 1/2 cups ice cubes

Mix the pretzels, margarine and 3 tablespoons sugar in a bowl. Press the pretzel mixture over the bottom of a 9x13-inch baking pan. Bake at 350 degrees for 6 minutes. Let stand until cool.

Beat the cream cheese, whipped topping and 1/2 cup sugar in a mixing bowl until smooth. Spread over the baked layer. Dissolve the gelatin in the boiling water in a heatproof bowl. Add the strawberries and ice cubes and stir until slightly thickened. Pour the gelatin mixture over the prepared layers. Chill, covered, until set. Cut into squares. Decrease the fat grams by using nonfat cream cheese.

Makes 9 (3x4-inch) servings

Nutrients Per Serving: Cal 499; Prot 6 g; Carbo 67 g; T Fat 24 g; (Saturated Fat 12 g); 42% Cal from Fat; Chol 28 mg; Fiber 2 g; Sod 528 mg; Calcium 30 mg

Carrots Gone Wild Salad

8 ounces baby carrots, peeled, shredded
2 medium Delicious apples, peeled, chopped
1/2 cup raisins
1/2 cup walnuts, finely chopped
2 tablespoons mayonnaise
1/2 teaspoon cinnamon

Combine the carrots, apples, raisins and walnuts in a bowl and mix well. Add the mayonnaise and cinnamon and mix well. Chill, covered, until serving time.

Serves 6

Nutrients Per Serving: Cal 176; Prot 2 g; Carbo 21 g; T Fat 10 g; (Saturated Fat 1 g); 50% Cal from Fat; Chol 3 mg; Fiber 3 g; Sod 40 mg; Calcium 28 mg

Oven Apples

4 small baking apples
2 tablespoons chopped pecans or walnuts
2 tablespoons raisins
1 teaspoon cinnamon

Cut the apples into halves; scoop out the cores. Arrange the apple halves cut side up in a baking dish. Combine the pecans, raisins and cinnamon in a bowl and mix well.

Spoon the pecan mixture into the apple halves. Bake, covered, at 350 degrees for 30 minutes. Serve warm, at room temperature or chilled for breakfast, lunch, dinner or as a snack.

Serves 8

Nutrients Per Serving: Cal 51; Prot <1 g; Carbo 10 g; T Fat 2 g; (Saturated Fat <1 g); 25% Cal from Fat; Chol 0 mg; Fiber 2 g; Sod <1 mg; Calcium 6 mg

Autumn is a great time to visit Western Maryland, where hardwood forests come alive with brilliant fall foliage. Hop aboard the "Autumn Leaves Special" train from Hagerstown to Thurmont or Hagerstown to Cumberland. Relax and enjoy the show, which is spectacular in mid-October! On your way home, stop for a basket or bushel of apples fresh from the orchards of Western Maryland.

Hot Cereal Surprise

1 cup cooked rolled oats
1 apple, chopped
1 cup 2% or fat-free milk
1/4 cup raisins, chopped dried apricots or dates
1/4 teaspoon cinnamon
1 to 2 tablespoons honey (optional)

Combine the oats, apple, 2% milk, raisins and cinnamon in a small saucepan and mix well. Stir in the honey. Cook over low heat for 5 to 10 minutes, stirring occasionally. Serve hot.

Makes 2 (1/2-cup) servings

Nutrients Per Serving: Cal 309; Prot 11 g; Carbo 58 g; T Fat 5 g; (Saturated Fat 2 g); 15% Cal from Fat; Chol 9 mg; Fiber 7 g; Sod 65 mg; Calcium 183 mg

Beanie Weenie Casserole

1 (30-ounce) can pork and beans
8 frankfurters, cut into 1/2-inch slices
2 tablespoons brown sugar

Pour the beans into a microwave-safe bowl. Stir in the frankfurters and brown sugar. Microwave, covered, until heated through, stirring once or twice during the process.

Serves 16

Nutrients Per Serving: Cal 150; Prot 6 g; Carbo 13 g; T Fat 9 g; (Saturated Fat 3 g); 52% Cal from Fat; Chol 18 mg; Fiber 3 g; Sod 554 mg; Calcium 34 mg

Rich Muffins

1 cup flour
1¹/2 teaspoons baking powder
¹/2 teaspoon salt
2¹/2 tablespoons margarine, softened
1¹/2 tablespoons sugar
¹/2 cup milk
1 egg, lightly beaten

Spray 6 muffins cups with nonstick cooking spray. Mix the flour, baking powder and salt. Combine the margarine and sugar in a bowl and mix until creamy. Add the flour mixture, milk and egg and mix just until moistened.

Fill the prepared muffin cups 2/3 full. Bake at 400 degrees for 20 to 25 minutes or until golden brown. Serve immediately. Double the recipe for a large crowd but use only 1 egg.

Makes 6 muffins

Nutrients Per Serving: Cal 156; Prot 4 g; Carbo 20 g; T Fat 6 g; (Saturated Fat 2 g); 37% Cal from Fat; Chol 38 mg; Fiber 1 g; Sod 392 mg; Calcium 101 mg

Almost Fried Ice Cream

2 cups frozen vanilla yogurt or lite ice cream
1¹/4 cups multigrain cereal with fruit and almonds, coarsely crushed
4 teaspoons honey
1 teaspoon cinnamon

Make four ¹/2-cup scoops of yogurt. Place the scoops in a shallow dish. Freeze, covered, for 30 minutes or until firm. Roll the scoops in the cereal. Return the ice cream balls to the dish. Freeze, covered, for 30 minutes or until firm.

Combine the honey and cinnamon in a small bowl. Drizzle some of the honey mixture over each ice cream ball just before serving.

Serves 4

Nutrients Per Serving: Cal 205; Prot 7 g; Carbo 44 g; T Fat <1 g; (Saturated Fat 0 g); 2% Cal from Fat; Chol 3 mg; Fiber 1 g; Sod 86 mg; Calcium 207 mg

Simple to prepare and quite satisfying, these muffins are a wonderful accompaniment to dinner, or add nuts and raisins and serve for breakfast. Innkeepers along the National Road must have offered similar choices to weary travelers. Completed in 1818 and extending from the Cumberland to the Ohio Valley, the National Road was a forerunner of today's interstates. Travelers and goods made their way from port cities like Baltimore to frontier settlements in the west using the National Road. Today, the National Freeway (I-68) carries interstate traffic west from Hancock and parallels the old National Road.

Snow Ice Cream

1 cup half-and-half
3/4 cup sugar
1 teaspoon vanilla extract
2 quarts packed clean snow
Pineapple tidbits (optional)
Sliced strawberries or other fruit (optional)
Chocolate syrup (optional)

Combine the half-and-half, sugar and vanilla in a bowl and mix until the sugar dissolves. Add the half-and-half mixture to the snow in a bowl and mix well. Scoop the snow ice cream into bowls. Top each serving with pineapple tidbits, strawberries and/or chocolate syrup. Serve immediately.

Serves 8

Nutrients Per Serving: Cal 112; Prot 1 g; Carbo 20 g; T Fat 3 g; (Saturated Fat 2 g); 27% Cal from Fat; Chol 11 mg; Fiber 0 g; Sod 12 mg; Calcium 32 mg

Frozen Banana Sandwiches

1 1/2 cups fat-free milk
1 (4-serving) package banana cream sugar-free instant pudding mix
8 ounces frozen fat-free whipped topping, thawed
1 cup miniature marshmallows
12 whole graham crackers, broken into 24 squares
1 1/2 bananas, thinly sliced

Combine the fat-free milk and pudding mix in a bowl and mix using package directions. Fold in the whipped topping and marshmallows.

Arrange 12 of the graham cracker squares on a baking sheet lined with foil. Layer each square with banana slices and a scant 1/4 cup of the pudding mixture. Top with the remaining graham cracker squares. Freeze, covered with plastic wrap, for 6 hours or until firm.

Makes 12 sandwiches

Nutrients Per Serving: Cal 136; Prot 3 g; Carbo 27 g; T Fat 2 g; (Saturated Fat <1 g); 10% Cal from Fat; Chol 1 mg; Fiber 1 g; Sod 159 mg; Calcium 42 mg

The children will be delighted with this simple recipe for Snow Ice Cream. When the weatherman predicts a snowfall, add half-and-half to the grocery list.

Dirt Cake with Worms

2 cups fat-free milk
1 (4-ounce) package chocolate instant pudding mix
1 (16-ounce) package chocolate sandwich cookies, crushed
8 ounces frozen whipped topping, thawed
Gummy worms (optional)

Pour the fat-free milk into a large bowl. Add the pudding mix and whisk until blended. Let stand for 5 minutes. Fold in 1/2 of the cookie crumbs and whipped topping.

Spoon the pudding mixture into a sterile ceramic flowerpot. Chill, covered, for 1 hour. Sprinkle with the remaining cookie crumbs. Garnish with gummy worms. You may serve in individual 7-ounce cups.

Makes 15 (1/2-cup) servings

Nutrients Per Serving: Cal 220; Prot 3 g; Carbo 32 g; T Fat 9 g; (Saturated Fat 4 g); 37% Cal from Fat; Chol 1 mg; Fiber 1 g; Sod 294 mg; Calcium 49 mg

Peanut Butter Fudge

3/4 cup peanut butter
1/2 cup light corn syrup
1/2 cup (1 stick) margarine, softened
1 teaspoon vanilla extract
1/2 teaspoon salt
4 cups confectioners' sugar

Combine the peanut butter, corn syrup, margarine, vanilla and salt in a mixing bowl. Beat until blended. Add the confectioners' sugar gradually, beating constantly until smooth.

Spread the peanut butter mixture in a 9x9-inch dish; flatten using a sheet of waxed paper. Chill, covered, until set. Cut into squares.

Makes 2 dozen squares

Nutrients Per Serving: Cal 178; Prot 2 g; Carbo 27 g; T Fat 8 g; (Saturated Fat 2 g); 38% Cal from Fat; Chol 0 mg; Fiber <1 g; Sod 139 mg; Calcium 5 mg

Slow-Cooker Apple Butter

8 cups canned applesauce
1 (12-ounce) can frozen apple juice concentrate
4 teaspoons cinnamon
1 1/2 teaspoons nutmeg
3/4 teaspoon ground cloves
1/2 teaspoon salt

Combine the applesauce and apple juice concentrate in a slow cooker and mix well. Cook on Low for 5 hours or until the volume is decreased by 1/2. Stir in the cinnamon, nutmeg, cloves and salt.

Cook for several more hours or to the consistency of apple butter. Spoon the apple butter into several small containers. Store in the refrigerator for up to 2 weeks. Store in the freezer for a longer storage period.

Makes 32 (2-tablespoon) servings

Nutrients Per Serving: Cal 45; Prot <1 g; Carbo 12 g; T Fat <1 g; (Saturated Fat <1 g); 2% Cal from Fat; Chol 0 mg; Fiber 1 g; Sod 40 mg; Calcium 8 mg

Playdough

1 cup flour
1/2 cup salt
2 teaspoons cream of tartar
1 cup water
1 teaspoon vegetable oil
Food coloring

Combine the flour, salt and cream of tartar in a saucepan and mix well. Stir in the water, oil and desired food coloring. Cook for 10 minutes or until the mixture adheres, stirring frequently. Let stand until cool. Store in an airtight container. The playdough is water soluble, making cleanup extremely simple.

Makes a fun day

Serve Slow-Cooker Apple Butter as a topping for toast, pancakes, or French toast. In Pennsylvania Dutch country, they serve Apple Butter on cottage cheese. Children can be involved in the measuring, mixing, and stirring, and the process can be spread over two days, adding spices on the second day. The house will smell wonderful!

Nutrient Content Claims

The food labeling regulations from the U.S. Food and Drug Administration spell out what terms may be used to describe the level of a nutrient in a food and how they can be used.

- **FREE.** This term means that a product contains no amount of, or only trivial amounts of, one or more of these components: fat, saturated fat, cholesterol, sodium, sugars, and calories. For example, "Calorie-free" means fewer than 5 calories per serving.

    low-fat: 3 g or less per serving

    low-saturated fat: 1 g or less per serving

    low-sodium: 140 mg or less per serving

    low-cholesterol: 20 mg or less and 2 g or less of saturated fat per serving

    low-calorie: 40 calories or less per serving.

Synonyms for low include "little," "few," "low source of," and "contains a small amount of."

- **HIGH.** The food contains 20 percent or more of the Daily Value for a particular nutrient in a serving.
- **GOOD SOURCE.** One serving of a food contains 10 to 19 percent of the Daily Value for a particular nutrient.
- **REDUCED.** The nutritionally altered product contains at least 25 percent less of a nutrient or of calories than the regular product. However, a reduced claim can't be made on a product if its reference food already meets the requirement for a "low" claim.
- **LIGHT.** The nutritionally altered product contains one-third fewer calories or half the fat of the reference food. If the food derives 50 percent or more of its calories from fat, the reduction must be 50 percent of the fat **OR** the sodium content of a low-calorie, low-fat food has been reduced by 50 percent. In addition, "light in sodium" may be used on food in which the sodium content has been reduced by at least 50 percent. The term "light" can be used to describe texture and color, as long as the label explains the intent—for example, "light brown sugar" and "light and fluffy."

The regulations also address claims that a meal or main dish is "free" of a nutrient, such as sodium or cholesterol, must meet the same requirements as those for individual foods. Other claims can be used under special circumstances. For example, "low-calorie" means the meal or main dish contains 120 calories or less per 100 grams. "Low-sodium" means the food has 140 mg or less per 100 g. "Low-cholesterol" means the food contains 20 mg cholesterol or less per 100 g and no more than 2 g saturated fat. "Light" means the meal or main dish is low-fat or low-calorie.

Adapted from the May 1999 U.S. Food and Drug Administration Backgrounder.

Dietary Guidelines for Americans

The Dietary Guidelines for Americans, developed jointly by the U.S. Departments of Agriculture (USDA) and Health and Human Services, provide recommendations for healthy Americans ages 2 and over about food choices that promote health and help reduce risk for chronic disease. The current guidelines of 2000 carry three basic messages:

Aim For Fitness
Build A Healthy Base
Choose Sensibly

By adhering to the following ten guidelines, you can promote your health and reduce your risk for certain diseases, such as heart disease, certain types of cancers, stroke, diabetes, and osteoporosis.

AIM FOR FITNESS
- Aim for a healthy weight
- Be physically active each day

BUILD A HEALTHY BASE
- Let the Pyramid guide your food choices
- Choose a variety of grains daily, especially whole grains
- Choose a variety of fruits and vegetables daily
- Keep food safe to eat

CHOOSE SENSIBLY
- Choose a diet that is low in saturated fat and cholesterol and moderate in total fat
- Choose beverages and foods to moderate your intake of sugars
- Choose and prepare foods with less salt
- If you drink alcoholic beverages, do so in moderation

Food Guide Pyramid—A Guide to Daily Food Choices

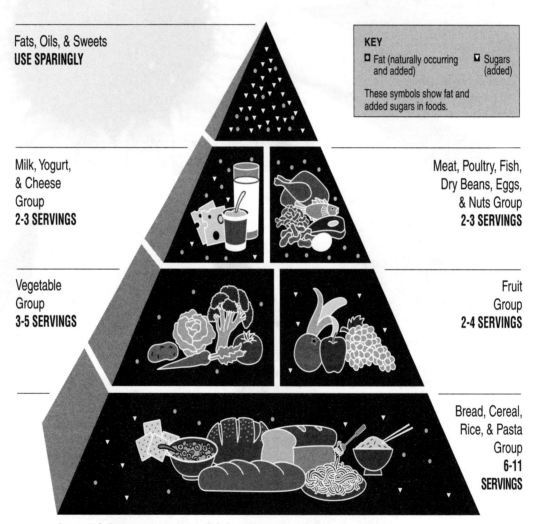

Fats, Oils, & Sweets
USE SPARINGLY

KEY
◘ Fat (naturally occurring and added)   ▽ Sugars (added)

These symbols show fat and added sugars in foods.

Milk, Yogurt, & Cheese Group
2-3 SERVINGS

Meat, Poultry, Fish, Dry Beans, Eggs, & Nuts Group
2-3 SERVINGS

Vegetable Group
3-5 SERVINGS

Fruit Group
2-4 SERVINGS

Bread, Cereal, Rice, & Pasta Group
6-11 SERVINGS

Source: U.S. Department of Agriculture/U.S. Department of Health and Human Services

What Counts as a Serving?

BREAD, CEREAL, RICE, AND PASTA GROUP (Grains Group)—whole grain and refined

- 1 slice of bread
- About 1 cup of ready-to-eat cereal
- 1/2 cup of cooked cereal, rice, or pasta

VEGETABLE GROUP

- 1 cup of raw leafy vegetables
- 1/2 cup of other vegetables—cooked or raw
- 3/4 cup of vegetable juice

FRUIT GROUP

- 1 medium apple, banana, orange, pear
- 1/2 cup of chopped, cooked, or canned fruit
- 3/4 cup of fruit juice

MILK, YOGURT, AND CHEESE GROUP (Milk Group)*

- 1 cup of milk** or yogurt**
- 1 1/2 ounces of natural cheese** (such as Cheddar)
- 2 ounces of processed cheese** (such as American)

MEAT, POULTRY, FISH, DRY BEANS, EGGS, AND NUTS GROUP (Meat and Beans Group)

- 2–3 ounces of cooked lean meat, poultry, or fish
- 1/2 cup of cooked dry beans# or 1/2 cup of tofu counts as 1 ounce of lean meat
- 2 1/2-ounce soyburger or 1 egg couns as 1 ounce of lean meat
- 2 tablespoons of peanut butter or 1/3 cup of nuts counts as 1 ounce of meat

NOTE: Many of the serving sizes given above are smaller than those on the Nutrition Facts Label. For example, 1 serving of cooked cereal, rice, or pasta is 1 cup of the label but only 1/2 cup for the Pyramid.

*This includes lactose-free and lactose-reduced milk products. One cup of soy-based beverage with added calcium is an option for those who prefer a non-dairy source of calcium.

**Choose fat-free or reduced-fat dairy products most often.

#Dry beans, peas, and lentils can be counted as servings in either the meat and beans group or the vegetable group. As a vegetable, 1/2 cup of cooked, dry beans counts as 1 serving. As a meat substitute, 1 cup of cooked, dry beans counts as 1 serving (2 ounces of meat).

Contributors

Michelle Albee

Lesa Amy

Barbara A. Bailey

Etrenda C. Banks

Cathleen Bilodeau

Pat Binko

Karen M. Bolderman

Kara Bolonda

Charlotte Booze

Lisa Brubaker

Marlene Butler

Emily Cartwright

Kelly M. Cervone

Katherine M. Chin

Susan Cottongim

Janet Debelius

Marie DeMarco

Judy Dzimiera

Noreen Eberly

Blenda Eckert

Mary Edmonds

Cathy Ferraro

Nancy Ferrone

Doris Fields

Judith Geggis

Sue Grandizio

Ellen Green

Lynn Greenberg

Asha Gullapalli

Pam Hartnett

Kelly Harvey

Sandra Hegelein

Julie Hickey

Nancy Horner

Traci Horwat

Nina P. Hoy

Darlene Jameson-Wheaton

Betty G. Johnson

Ruth B. Kershner

Amy B. Kraemer

Tracey Leef

Mary Ann LeMay

Jane Libby

Del Lloyd

Carol Loomis

Sheila Mackertich

Liat Mackey

Alicia Magday

Phyllis McCarron

Kimberly Menges

Carol R. Miller

Ginger Muscalli

Eulalia Muschik

Sandy Niblett

Elaine Pardoe

Siony Placiente

Dah Rhow

Janet Roseland

Cheryl Rosenfeld

Cindy Sileo

Elaine Smith

Theresa Stahl

Arlene Swantko

Robin Thomas

Joan Todd

Andrea C. Troutner

Brie Turner-McGrievy

Connie Webster

Jennifer Wilson

Kathy Wool

Joanne Zacharias

Resources

www.dnr.state.md.us/mdmap.html—provided by the Department of Natural Resources, this site furnishes information about Maryland's state parks.

www.marylandapples.org—learn about varieties of apples grown in Maryland; includes a list of Maryland orchards categorized by county.

www.marylandracing.com—provides information on the Preakness Stakes and other Pimlico events.

www.mdarchives.state.md.us.—the historical agency and permanent records repository for the state.

www.mdisfun.org—the Maryland Office of Tourism Development publishes the "Maryland Calendar of Events" the official calendar of events for the state.

www.nal.usda.gov/fnic/foodcomp—this website of the Food and Nutrition Information Center of the National Agricultural Library at the Untied States Department of Agriculture contains detailed reports of the nutrient content of your favorite foods.

www.marylandwine.com—a good resource to learn about grapes or locate the wineries in the state.

www.sha.state.md.us/oed/bywaysprogram/htm—the Maryland State Highway Administration offers a Scenic Byways program. Use this website to find out about the Scenic Byway Directional Signs found along roads throughout the state and to order the Maryland Scenic Byways Map or the accompanying 192-page booklet.

Bibliography

Arkin, Frieda. *The Complete Book of Kitchen Wisdom.* Galahad Books. New York, NY. 1993.

Arnett, Earl, Brugger, Robert J., and Papenfuse, Edward C. *Maryland—A New Guide to the Old Line State, Second Edition.* The Johns Hopkins University Press. Baltimore, MD. 1999.

Atticks, Kevin M. *Discovering Maryland Wineries—A Travel Guide to Maryland's Wine Country.* Resonant Publishing. Baltimore, MD. 1999.

Carey, George G. *Maryland Folklore.* Tidewater Publishers. Centreville, MD. 1989.

Duyff, Roberta Larson. *The American Dietetic Association's Complete Food & Nutrition Guide.* Chronimed Publishing. Minneapolis, MN. 1996.

Ecenbarger, William. *Walkin' the Line—A Journey from past to present along the Mason-Dixon.* M. Evans and Company, Inc. New York, NY. 2000.

Kaessmann, Beta, Manakee, Harold Randall, and Wheeler, Joseph L. *My Maryland.* The Maryland Historical Society. Baltimore, MD. 1955.

Manakee, Harold R. *Indians of Early Maryland.* Maryland Historical Society. Baltimore, MD. 1981.

Marck, John T. *Maryland—The Seventh State, A History, Fourth Edition.* Creative Impressions, Ltd. Glen Arm, MD. 1998.

McGee, Harold. *On Food and Cooking.* Macmillan Publishing Company. New York, NY. 1984.

Porter, Frank W. III. *Maryland Indians Yesterday and Today.* Museum and Library of Maryland History, The Maryland Historical Society. Baltimore, MD. 1983.

RESI—Research and Consulting Towson University and The Maryland Department of Business and Economic Development. *2000 Maryland Statistical Abstract.*

Rogers, Barbara Radcliffe, and Rogers, Stillman. *Adventure Guide to The Chesapeake Bay.* Hunter Publishing. Edison, New Jersey. 2001.

Seldon, Lynn. *Country Roads of Maryland and Delaware, Second Edition.* Country Roads Press division of NTC Publishing. Chicago, IL. 1999.

Stieff, Frederick Philip. *Eat, Drink, & Be Merry in Maryland.* The Johns Hopkins University Press. Baltimore, MD. 1998.

Tantillo, Tony, and Gugino, Sam. *Eat Fresh, Stay Healthy.* Simon and Schuster Macmillan Company. New York, NY. 1997.

Wilson, Richard, and Bridner, Jack. *Maryland—Its Past and Present.* Maryland Historical Press. Lanham, MD. 1997.

Index

Order Information

EXPLORE THE TASTES OF MARYLAND
From the Mountains to the Sea

Maryland Dietetic Association
P.O. Box 1151
Brooklandville, Maryland 21022
1-800-794-1152

Please send _____ copies of *Explore the Tastes of Maryland* at $19.95 each $ _____

Maryland residents add 5% sales tax $ _____

Shipping and handling at $4.95 each $ _____

TOTAL $ _____

_____
Name

_____
Street Address

_____
City   State   Zip

_____
Telephone

Method of Payment: [   ] Discover   [   ] MasterCard   [   ] VISA

[   ] Check payable to the Maryland Dietetic Association

_____
Account Number   Expiration Date

_____
Signature

Photocopies will be accepted.